Corporate Interiors

No. 10

Corporate Interiors
No. 10

Roger Yee

Opposite: Paul Hastings Janofsky & Walker, LLC **Design firm:** AECOM **Photography:** Joe Aker/Aker Zvonkovic Photography

Corporate Interiors No. 10

302 Fifth Avenue • New York, NY 10001
Tel: 212.279.7000 • Fax: 212.279.7014

www.visualreference.com

PUBLISHER	Larry Fuersich
	larry@visualreference.com
EDITORIAL DIRECTOR	Roger Yee
	rhtyee@gmail.com
CREATIVE ART DIRECTOR	Martina Parisi
	martina@visualreference.com
PRODUCTION MANAGER	John Hogan
	johnhvrp@yahoo.com
CONTROLLER	Angie Goulimis
	angie@visualreference.com

Copyright © 2010 by Visual Design Books, Inc.

Library of Congress Cataloging in Publication Data: Corporate Interiors No. 10

ISBN 13: 978-0-9825989-4-8
ISBN 10: 0-9825989-4-7

Distributors to the trade in the United States and Canada
Innovative Logistics
575 Prospect Street
Lakewood, NJ 08701
732.363.5679

Distributors outside the United States and Canada
HarperCollins International
10 East 53rd Street
New York, NY 10022-5299

Exclusive distributor in China
Beijing Designerbooks Co., Ltd.
B-0619, No.2 Building, Dacheng International Center
78 East 4th Ring Middle Road
Chaoyang District, Beijing 100022, P.R. China
Tel: 0086(010)5962-6195 Fax: 0086(010)5962-6193
E-mail: info@designerbooks.net www.designerbooks.net

Printed and bound in China

Book Design: Martina Parisi

The paper on which this book is printed contains
recycled content to support a sustainable world.

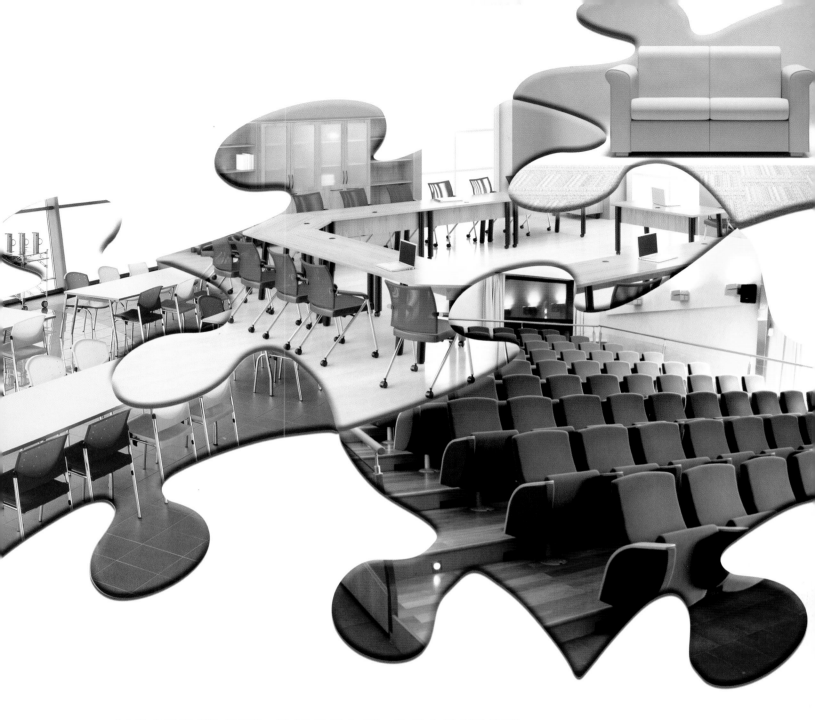

WHEREVER PEOPLE CONNECT ...

Finding the right fit where people and product unite to create a dynamic space can prove to be a challenging activity, but not for Dauphin. Wherever people connect we provide innovative furnishing solutions to increase creativity and collaboration. Our various products are part of the bigger picture, they enable people to thrive and connect in today's interactive environments.

INNOVATIVE FURNISHINGS FOR DYNAMIC SPACES

Contents

What Can Business Learn from Design Today?

Design matters to business now more than ever before, and a conversation with a distinguished principal of one of the nation's most successful design firms reveals why

So it's come to this: The wolf is at the door, the enemy has encircled the citadel, the house is on fire. To paraphrase a memorable line from the 1989 Ivan Reitman film *Ghostbusters,* "Who ya gonna call?" Business leaders grappling with the global recession will surely not place that first call to their architects or interior designers. But if they were to spend a few minutes with a seasoned professional designer such as architect Walter A. Hunt, Jr., FAIA, vice chairman of Gensler, that second or third call might surprise them. "Design is a holistic process," Hunt explains. "Design looks at why people use space to achieve their goals and what they want space to accomplish—not just how space can be shaped to suit them."

When corporate executives understand that design can be wielded as a strategic tool to manage change, they see office design in an entirely different light. "New offices enable organizations to catch up on the latest thinking about business management, corporate strategy and human resources," Hunt observes, "by putting that thinking into immediate action." He likens well-designed workspace to intellectual property, because it positions people to excel by equipping them with the environment and tools to complete their tasks most effectively. Though he wishes more business decision makers would grasp the true power of design, he is encouraged that fresh examples keep appearing in America and the world at large.

To back his observation, Hunt refers to enlightened executives such as Daniel Vasella, chairman and former CEO of Novartis, who develop superior corporate facilities to foster innovative thinking and breakthrough products. (Vasella launched the still ongoing conversion of a former manufacturing center in Basel, Switzerland into a brilliant administrative and R&D campus for Novartis.) Among the revelations about design that executives may not realize are such pearls as: Good design doesn't have to cost more than mediocrity; office design can produce measurable benefits; introducing amenities to stimulate interaction may not require allocating more space; and the quality of a company's facilities describes the company accurately to staff and public alike.

And what can business learn from design in 2010? "Design is prepared not just to solve problems," Hunt declares, "but to create opportunities." While design is rightly concerned with how a company has utilized space in the past and where it currently conducts its activities, it is also interested in what the company wants to be in the future, and the physical space it would need to attain its ideal. "Fortunately, business people will find the design process is not a subjective thing," Hunt adds. "We take you through a comprehensive learning process so you'll know what to expect." What business leaders expect in 2010 can be seen in the following pages of CORPORATE INTERIORS. It's our 10th Anniversary issue, and we hope you'll find the new projects by many of America's leading design firms as inspiring as we do.

Roger Yee
Editor

immix™

verb to mix in; blend; mingle **noun** a modular bench from VERSTEEL

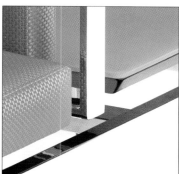
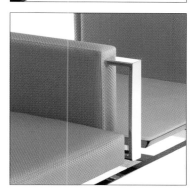

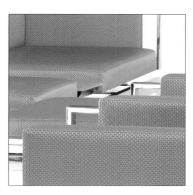
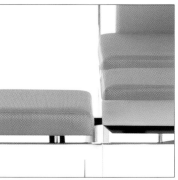

VERSTEEL®

Call **800 876 2120** or visit **versteel.com**

Occasionally even the most beautiful
objects have to bask in reflected glory.

Talo, cable suspension mounted luminaires
for direct and indirect fluorescent lighting,
using T5 fluorescent bulbs.
Design, Neil Poulton.

Artemide®
ARCHITECTURAL
THE HUMAN LIGHT.®

It's Facetime

Why business still needs the office in a global, digital economy

By Roger Yee

Creating no less than a whole life experience for employees, Nokia has placed a Town Center in its BDA Site's open atrium, in Beijing, China, one of numerous focal points for group activity.

With Walmart customers devouring 10 percent of China's exports, it's tempting to speculate about whether the last American leaving the office will even have time to turn out the lights. But architects and interior designers serving the corporate world see a very different picture. From coast to coast, they are working with organizations determined to survive, prosper and grow, and developing new kinds of workplace environments to help their clients' employees reach their goals.

"I'm not of the opinion that the office is on life support," says Joe Connell, a principal of Perkins+Will. "In fact, there's more emphasis now on effectiveness than economy in office design. Businesses need offices that work for them."

On the occasion of the publishing of its 10th anniversary volume, CORPORATE INTERIORS takes a guided tour of the contemporary office to examine its status in the digital age: where it excels as a unique and valuable facility, what trends in office design say about current business practice, and how its evolving form and function affect businesses and communities. Our knowledgeable tour guides include Connell of Perkins+Will, in Chicago, Jo Heinz, president and CEO of Staffelbach in Houston, and Amanda Kaleps, a principal of Wolcott Architecture Interiors in Culver City, California. For business leaders and the architects and interior designers who serve them, the discussions that follow should be a lively, intriguing and—given the ongoing turmoil of the global recession—uplifting journey.

It's no accident why Logica's Houston, TX office has designed its open office area, shown here with hoteling wall, to keep communications as open as possible: It stimulates problem solving.

GIANNI

ALLIANCE

TRADITIONAL METHODS, CONTEMPORARY SOLUTIONS

From the Boardroom to the General Office
Functional, Elegant, Timeless
Office Furniture in Wood

www.gianniinc.com

4615 W. Roosevelt Rd., Cicero, Il. 60804   Tel.708.863.6696   Fax.708.863.4071
Showroom 10.124 Merchandise Mart - Chicago

If you hire brainy people, you may offer them such inducements to gather together as the Café at Sapient, Boston, MA, an attractive alternative to employees' individual office "neighborhoods."

Where the modern office excels in a sea of iPhones

While powerful new digital ways to work are proliferating across the global economy, businesses are repeatedly discovering there is still no place like the office. Not only do their personnel find compelling reasons to use offices, but offices continue to play strategic roles in business and public life, and alternative offices supplement rather than replace conventional offices. In fact, the case for offices is reinforced by laptops, smart phones and other mobile technologies.

An important key to success today is interaction, cooperation and collaboration within groups and between groups that produce innovative thinking and breakthrough ideas. Because business activity increasingly extends beyond time zones and borderlines, the network of people involved in a single project can stretch far beyond the walls of the largest office. Why should the office matter when a team meeting can be convened at the touch of a Blackberry?

"Teamwork among independent individuals and groups doesn't thrive without a trusted network," Connell maintains. "Networks are built on mutual understanding, personal chemistry and shared experiences. To establish these values, you need regular face-to-face encounters, and that's what offices do best. Teleconferencing comes close, but it doesn't replace offices."

Similarly, day-to-day group activity thrives in offices, giving individuals who can perform their private tasks at home or Starbucks appropriate settings with space, equipment and support services not easily replicated elsewhere. Confidentiality is another justification for offices, whenever trade secrets and sensitive legal and financial issues are at stake. Furthermore, as Connell declares, "People still like to belong to tangible organizations. Space matters. We enjoy working in the presence of like-minded colleagues. And in difficult times like these, it's a lot better facing problems together. If you're young, you can learn so much by observing how more experienced colleagues deal with difficult situations."

Interestingly, offices remain vital physical and symbolic images of companies, making their form and function important to a wide circle of stakeholders. "Everything sends messages, positive and negative," Connell insists. "That's why many companies now brand their offices along the lines of classic brand building, eliminating negative values, building awareness and acceptance, and finally establishing preference."

Alternative offices have proven their value to business, Connell confirms, but have demonstrated their limitations as well. "Corporate America has done lots of outsourcing," he says. "This has led to smaller facilities located in central business districts that are highly accessible to employees and task-driven rather than status-driven. Companies are constructing fewer monster campuses and shifting from owning to leasing. When it comes to satellite offices and telecommuting from home, employers now recognize both their convenience and inconvenience. Working from home can be great for parents of young children, but home is often a lousy office for the same reason it's a great escape from the office."

What current trends in office design say about business in 2010

Amidst the unstable markets, troubled companies and job losses resulting from the global recession, the office takes on an even greater importance as a source of stability, support and identity,

A key to success today is encouraging interaction among employees that produces innovative thinking, and the Drum Room at Kosmos Energy, Dallas, TX, offers a stylish if informal venue.

according to Jo Heinz of Staffelbach. "Office design communicates to employees and visitors what a company stands for," she declares. "Whether you're stationed at a desk or on the road, the office now acts as a 24/7 home base."

This pragmatic approach to the workplace shows up in various telling ways. For example, job tasks rather than organizational rankings increasingly determine floor area, spatial configuration, furnishings and finishes in office design, resulting in spaces that are bigger or smaller than before—and more or less elaborate—because the business functions they serve demand it. Few areas of the office are now spared from this kind of value engineering, including executive offices.

Demand for flexibility has brought standardized spaces designed for multiple functions or easy reconfiguration, Heinz reports. (Even boardrooms incorporate adaptable features to serve a diversity of users when boards aren't meeting.) The need to help the workforce sustain a high level of productivity is often ensured by applying sustainable design principles—winning LEED Silver, Gold and Platinum certification at times—to construction techniques, materials selection, HVAC, lighting, energy, water, acoustics and ergonomics.

Amenities once considered frivolous or extravagant, such as coffee bars, employee lounges and emergency daycare, have assumed a new strategic importance. "Layoffs make your remaining core workers more important than ever," Heinz observes, "inspiring companies to include amenities in the workplace to help maintain morale, focus and commitment. After all, you're asking fewer people to do more work."

Consider the way businesses currently develop and use the following key office components.

Reception: "It's the first brand statement you see when you walk into an office," Heinz says. "Because each organization's identity is as unique as a fingerprint, executives want reception areas to declare what their companies stand for. Here's where visitors first meet their hosts, and first impressions count."

Conference room: "Heightened security typically results in conference rooms that are centrally located or positioned just off the reception area," Heinz indicates. "The rooms themselves are turning into highly functional, multi-purpose facilities equipped for

A leader in the residential textile industry, Donghia + Bergamo, Mt. Vernon, NY, proudly shares its heritage of design and craftsmanship with employees and visitors in the boardroom.

training, lunch and special events—not just conferences."

Private office: "Here's where the greatest change has occurred," Heinz believes. "Employers see private offices and email cutting off interaction and stifling communication. As a result, private offices are smaller, non-hierarchical and more accessible. They're less status symbols than before, since IT lets us work anywhere."

Open workstation: "Many workers, especially younger ones, are thrilled that we're getting away from the vertical panels in open workstations," Heinz is discovering. (Older colleagues have mixed feelings.) "Low barriers foster better communications, even if designers must balance normal conversations with ambient noise."

Lounge: "Businesses now recognize that there are different ways of working besides sitting at a desk," Heinz says. "Lounges are springing up as multi-purpose facilities to encourage informal gatherings for problem solving and brainstorming, training, conferences, breakouts: You name it and the lounge can do it."

Food service and other amenities: "McKinsey has found that group activity is converging on food and media," Heinz has learned. "Companies are using this insight to create amenity spaces that resemble airline clubs and act as refuges from the 24/7 workday. They want them to be every bit as good as the local coffee shop."

If the traditional categories of office facilities are yielding to more flexible or even ambiguous ones, Heinz is not surprised, since the once monolithic work force is becoming a heterogeneous one

Coming to Phoenix, AZ from out of state, MidFirst Bank has created a Southwestern style bank lobby with stone fireplace lounge and teller stations to make customers feel instantly at home.

where full-time staff must make room for part-timers, contract workers, visiting employees from other locations, and consultants. Another reason for the new openness to change is the inability to predict the future of global economic conditions or technological advances. "Clients who once drew up five- and ten-year plans admit they're not sure what lies beyond the next six months," Heinz confides. "How you design for this is one of our greatest challenges."

How the modern office affects business and society

Business leaders have long regarded offices as problematic expenditures, requiring major investments that can be seen either as strategic assets or overhead liabilities. Part of the problem, according to Amanda Kaleps of Wolcott Architecture Interiors, is the corporate world's continuing inability to measure the benefits of office design, a shortcoming acknowledged by the design

Among the many ways to raise morale, focus and commitment among workers is to bring daylight and views deep inside, as can be seen at the open office area of Société Générale, Chicago, IL.

Branding the office tells staff and customers what an organization stands for, so Karl Storz Endoscopy-America Inc., Santa Monica, CA, uses the view from the stair to face a memorable history wall.

community. "We usually focus on productivity," she says. "It's difficult for designers to claim full credit for this, however." Indeed, there is a wealth of motivations for raising productivity that transcend design, technology and even economics.

Good design often correlates with human resources goals, as corporate executives willingly concede. "Design can directly influence such HR variables as job recruitment, job retention and sick days," Kaleps notes. "The design of an office can help a company reinforce its brand and stand out from the competition. Tearing down walls can encourage people to speak to each other directly rather than resort to texting or email."

Over the long term, Kaleps finds more and more companies agreeing with the "Google model" of office design, which aims to create spaces where people want to stay for long periods of time. "It helps in drafting a work-life philosophy for an organization to have a work environment that represents an effective and comfortable place that is distinctly different from home," she asserts. "There is a role for the alternative office, but clients define it carefully to get the right people and functions involved. Even as

individual offices or workstations reduce their floor area, new group areas add to the total. Organizations see the value of having these 'neighborhoods' and 'communities' within their offices to get employees to interact, connecting Boomers and Millennials, and transferring knowledge from veterans to newcomers."

How the office connects with its surrounding community remains an issue focused primarily on cost and convenience, as Kaleps and her colleagues find in serving businesses in greater Los Angeles. Culture factors in as well. "For clients who are in the entertainment industry," she explains, "Century City is where the moguls are, and they want to be there too. Otherwise, many clients look at rent first and foremost."

The situation is improving nonetheless. "Companies want to be where the talent pool is attracted," she says. "If the people they want to hire like walking to work or taking mass transit, enjoy having good nearby restaurants and shopping at lunch hour, and convenience to entertainment and cultural attractions after work, more clients are responding to them."

Complex and evolving as the modern office is, the experiences of Joe Connell, Jo Heinz and Amanda Kaleps clearly place it at the center of the business landscape for the foreseeable future. Where it is going may be impossible to predict. Yet wherever the corporate world goes, the office will surely follow in a vital, supporting role. ✆

The perfect light equation

From simple utilitarian structures to grand architectural masterpieces, The Lighting Quotient combines serious performance with artistic elegance.

Learn more about our elliptipar and tambient divisions at TheLightingQuotient.com.

Corcoran Williamsburg
Architect: cubellis a/r environetics
Lighting Design: zeroLUX Lighting Design
Photography: Courtesy cubellis
a/r environetics

elliptipar
There is no equal™

tambient
Green in any color®

THE LIGHTING **QUOTIENT**

AECOM

515 South Flower Street, 8th Floor • Los Angeles, CA 90071 • 213.593.8100
800 Douglas Entrance • North Tower, 2nd Floor • Coral Gables, Florida 33134 • 305.444.4691
2777 East Camelback Road, Suite 200 • Phoenix, AZ 85016 • 602.337.2700
3101 Wilson Blvd, Suite 900 • Arlington, VA 22201, USA • 703.682.4900
10 South Jefferson Street, Suite 1600 • Roanoke, VA 24011 • 540.857.3100
448 Viking Drive, Suite 145 • Virginia Beach, VA 23452 • 757.306.4000
Americas • Europe • Asia • Middle East • Africa • Australia • New Zealand
www.aecom.com

AECOM

Paul Hastings Janofsky & Walker, LLP
San Diego, California

Serving clients in such diverse industries as biotechnology, electronics, telecommunications and retail, the San Diego office of Paul Hastings Janofsky & Walker does more than extend this leading international law firm's geography. Paul Hastings' new, two-and-a-half-floors, 50,000-square-foot space at

La Jolla Commons, designed by AECOM, simultaneously explores green design and thoughtfully interprets newly enforced, more stringent building code. The focal point of the contemporary office, which includes partner, attorney and associate private offices, paralegal and secretary workstations

and such support facilities as a high-density filing area, lunchroom and case rooms, is the highly visible, half-floor Conferencing Center, adjacent to the building's main entrance at street level. Since Paul Hastings was the LEED Silver-certified office tower's first tenant, AECOM had flexibility in developing the

Conferencing Center as an innovative design showcase, enclosing conference rooms in an organic, high-technology glass shape that becomes opaque for greater privacy when needed. The development of complex details, such as the wood ceiling system, and the electrostatic glazing panels, required both

AECOM's technical expertise and multiple discussions with the San Diego Building Department to ensure code and seismic compliance.

Above far left: Reception

Above left: Glass in clear mode revealing conference room

Left: Seating in hallway

Opposite: Conference room entrance

Photography: Joe Aker/Aker Zvonkovic Photography

AECOM

Loyola Marymount University
William H. Hannon Library
Los Angeles, California

Once a quiet sanctum for books and scholars, the university library is now a technology-powered resource center where students study in collaborative spaces, as seen in Los Angeles at Loyola Marymount University's dramatic new, three-story (plus basement), 120,000-square-foot William H. Hannon Library. The Hannon Library, comprising reading rooms, group study rooms, collaborative study spaces, 24-hour study area, media lounge, stacks, café and outdoor dining terrace, has been designed by AECOM to give scholars access to information in every medium and to provide a variety of venues for individual and group activity. To simplify its organization, the building locates public access areas in its dominant cylindrical form, and places back of house functions in its ancillary rectangular masses, employing the intersection of circle and square at the center as the point of reference for each floor. The design exemplifies user friendliness, thanks to such features as WiFi connectivity, 24 group study rooms where display monitors and computer hook-ups promote collaborative learning, floor-to-ceiling whiteboards and dry erase markers, and furnishings designed for utility and comfort. Praising the outcome, Loyola Marymount's president, Robert Lawton, S.J., declares, "In its physical attributes, this building speaks to the very best the university can be."

Right: Exterior at main entry

Below: Reading room

Opposite, clockwise starting top left: Central staircase, café, information commons, group study room, lobby,

Photography: Tim Griffiths

AECOM

Altria Group
Richmond, Virginia

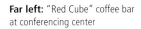

Far left: "Red Cube" coffee bar at conferencing center

Left: Open café opposite meeting rooms

Center far left: Annex branch of credit union

Center left: Dining room

Bottom left: Meeting rooms on typical floor

Below: Lobby

Photography: Nick Merrick/ Hedrich Blessing

Altria Group's headquarters in Richmond, Virginia has expanded its operations by adding a second building to its campus. The Annex, an eight level, 200,000 square foot structure designed by AECOM, provides complementary amenities and services to the employees of Altria, the parent company of Philip Morris as well as John Middleton Company, and US Smokeless Tobacco Company. Consisting of private offices, open plan offices, conference and team collaborative rooms, employee coffee and lounge areas, cafeteria with Servery, indoor and outdoor dining, classroom and conference center, multi-purpose room, coffee bar, credit union bank and escalator, the Annex establishes a high level of design and finishes to affirm its importance and update its accommodations. The three lower levels provide service functions, placing classrooms, credit union bank on the basement level, and dining facility, multi-purpose room, shipping and receiving and mail operations on the next two floors, while staff functions fill the remaining five floors. Color, materials, furnishings and lighting interact to link the Annex environment with the Headquarters building, evoking the main structure's classic Modernism, right down to the black stone and white terrazzo lobby that reprises the Headquarters building's signature look.

AECOM The Annenberg Space for Photography
Los Angeles, California

What could better serve a gallery devoted to exploring print and digital photography than an interior design influenced by a camera's inner workings? That's why the one-floor, 10,000-square-foot Annenberg Space for Photography in Los Angeles, designed by AECOM, features a central, circular digital gallery that evokes a convex lens, and places it beneath a ceiling with a shape reminiscent of a lens's aperture. Developing this concept further, the design exploits the Greek origin of the word "photograph" or "drawing with light" by letting light lead visitors along a winding photographic journey. Natural light transitions to artificial light before concluding at a completely contained area where darkness replaces light and digital imagery replaces print. Aside from its imagery, the facility serves visitors and staff with exceptional utility, flexibility and style. The entry gallery, for example, introduces print imagery below a curved soffit resembling a camera's film advancer that beckons visitors inside. Administrative space can be opened to enlarge the main digital gallery or enclosed for private functions. There is even a gallery boasting a professional kitchen, driven by the desire for an intimate space for workshops, brainstorming and dialogue, since "the best conversations occur in the kitchen."

Below: Central circular digital gallery
Top right: Entry gallery
Right: Display
Below right: Gallery space with kitchen
Photography: Tim Street-Porter

Aref & Associates

100 N. Sepulveda Blvd., Suite 100 • El Segundo, CA 90245 • 310.414.1000 • 310.414.1099 (F)

www.aref.com

Aref & Associates

Wells Fargo Center
Los Angeles, California

When Wells Fargo Center opened in the Bunker Hill section of downtown Los Angeles in 1983, its two angular granite, steel and glass-clad office towers, originally designed by Skidmore, Owings & Merrill, became instant landmarks. Today, the complex, consisting of the 54-story, 1.39 million-square-foot Wells Fargo Tower, 45-story, the 1.14 million-square-foot KPMG Tower, and the three-story glass atrium connecting them, continues to win awards and retain its upscale, Class-A status. To maintain the prestige of Wells Fargo Tower, Maguire Properties, the largest owner, developer, and manager of Class A office properties in Southern California, recently retained Aref & Associates to rebrand the building with a fresh yet timeless design for its main lobby. Working

Top left: Entrance
Left: Elevator lobby
Opposite: Elevator lobby
Photography: Paul Bielenberg

Aref & Associates

closely with Maguire, the design team created a crisp, contemporary image in white and red—using Italian Piana Carrara marble, Neoparies crystallized glass stone, Mt. Airy granite, gray birds-eye maple, Starfire glass and custom handmade rugs—that is illuminated by a sophisticated lighting scheme to capture its bold look. The new lobby makes sense for Maguire as well as its property, since the company takes pride in a portfolio highlighted by premier buildings of enduring quality designed by some of the nation's leading architects. Construction was carried out while the building was fully occupied through a meticulous staging of crews, materials and activities. Although tenants and visitors never lost a day's business owing to the renovation, they will surely be admiring the results for many years to come.

Below: Main lobby
Opposite top left and right: Elevator lobby
Opposite bottom: Concierge desk

Aref & Associates

Pacific Arts Plaza
Costa Mesa, California

For organizations seeking the business, cultural and entertainment center of California's Orange County, Pacific Arts Plaza, in Costa Mesa, is an ideal location. This 827,000-square-foot, Class-A office campus features two 15-story buildings, one eight-story building and one five-story building, all designed by Albert C. Martin & Associates, a 1.6-acre outdoor plaza and sculpture garden, designed by distinguished artist Isamu Noguchi, and such nearby amenities as the Orange County Performing Arts Center, South Coast Plaza mall, and numerous dining options. The challenge for Aref & Associates, retained by Maguire Properties to design a new and more appealing lobby for one of the 15-story buildings, was to introduce an open, light and airy space that would define the entry, connect the development on the north side with the Performing Arts Center and on the south side with the Noguchi Garden, and complement the building's sleek glass façade. The superbly detailed solution, beginning with a stone and glass portal that leads to a warm, soothing, contemporary interior of marble, limestone, glass, figured European ash and Zebrano wood illuminated by direct and indirect lighting featuring elegant pendant fixtures over the entry, makes Pacific Arts Plaza as compelling as the activity surrounding it.

Above: Entrance portal

Above left: Lobby and elevators

Left: View from concierge desk to entry foyer

Opposite: Evening view of entrance portal

Photography: Paul Bielenberg

Aref & Associates

Boston Consulting Group, Detroit Office
Troy, Michigan

Renowned for working with leading Fortune500 Firms around the globe, Boston Consulting Group recently opened a Detroit Office, its twenty-second North American office, in Troy, Michigan. The workspace housing Detroit consultants & staff not only supports their effort, it illustrates how the international strategy and general management consulting firm simultaneously becomes part of the local community while sharing the values of the firm's global network. Designed by Aref & Associates, the award-winning, 10,000-square-foot office, occupying one floor of a 14-story building along Detroit's northern business corridor, comprises private offices, administrative workstations, conference and team rooms, "commons" lounge and production center. Although the facility is organized around the consultants' private offices, it feels open, warm and inviting because partitions incorporate large expanses of glass, teamwork areas are attractive, and public spaces provide memorable experiences for employees and visitors alike. Such materials as European ash trim, English sycamore casegoods, Neoparies crystallized glass stone and Starfire glass acknowledge the firm's global identity. Yet details like the "enclave" in the reception area and the front end of a 1957 Chevrolet in the "commons" lounge celebrate the cultural phenomenon known as the American Road.

Top left: Seating area with "enclave" in reception area

Top right: Reception area showing reception desk

Above middle: Main conference room

Above: Commons

Photography: Paul Bielenberg

Conant Architects

315 Madison Avenue • New York, NY 10017 • 646.865.1200 • 646.865.1377 (F)

www.conantarchitects.com

Conant Architects

The Wallace Foundation
New York, New York

Right: View from elevator lobby into reception
Far right: Knowledge Center
Below: Open plan area
Below right: Breakout room
Bottom: Central reception
Bottom right: Lunch alcove
Photography: Andrea Brizzi

Recognized nationwide for its involvement in educational and cultural programs, the Wallace Foundation traces its origins a half century back to the philanthropic efforts of DeWitt and Lila Acheson Wallace, founders of The Reader's Digest Association. In changing to a team-based approach to its mission, the Foundation recently retained Conant Architects to design an appropriate new workplace in midtown Manhattan. The organization's new, one-floor, 30,000-squarefoot environment for 95 staff members succeeds not only in creating an effective, team-based workplace, but also in developing a high-quality environment on a stringent budget. Various design elements leverage the budget in inventive yet inexpensive ways. For example, though the floor plan reflects a conventional configuration in the reception area, private offices, open workstations, conference rooms, lunchroom and support spaces, the Knowledge Center, the Foundation's multi-media resource center, highlights the orthogonal composition with a cylindrical lunch alcove. Similarly, the color scheme matches the Foundation's iconic blue with cool white and warm anigre wood to project a fresh, dynamic image. Potentially intrusive cylindrical columns are transformed into book ends or featured as freestanding sculptural elements. Like the Foundation itself, the space convincingly shows that ideas count more than money in changing the world.

Conant Architects

Thomson Reuters
New York, New York

To design a new headquarters for the merger of Thomson Corporation and Reuters Group to form Thomson Reuters, the world's largest international multimedia news agency, Conant Architects recognized that integrating media tools with the workplace would be mandatory. That's why the one-floor, 30,000-square-foot facility enables company executives working here or anywhere else worldwide to stay in touch with all corporate activities at all times. Located in New York's bustling Times Square, the 30-person environment excels as a seamless integration of architecture and information technology. Like a high-tech machine, it promotes video conferencing virtually everywhere, aided by lighting, acoustics and security systems calibrated to support constant communications. Yet the space representing "light through a camera lens," aesthetically inspired by the building's curve, also functions as a sunny, spacious and comfortable setting. From the reception area to the executive offices, conference center (housing the boardroom), and cooking kitchen, a sophisticated interior of cherry wood, glass, fabric-clad acoustical panels and fine contemporary furnishings in traditional finishes gives executives world class accommodations. Better yet, the curving fin wall of cherry wood fins and glass that dominates the space simultaneously brings daylight deep inside and keeps Thomson Reuters in direct visual contact with the world.

Above: Boardroom vestibule

Above right: Executive office

Right: Primary corridor with fin wall

Lower right: Boardroom with retractable panels at screen

Left: Reception

Photography: Oleg March

Conant Architects Donghia + Bergamo
Mount Vernon, New York

Donghia and Bergamo, two furniture and textile industry icons, have merged headquarters and administrative functions as Donghia + Bergamo while keeping brands and customer contacts separate, gathering 80 employees and various operations under one roof in Mount Vernon, New York, and displaying the transformative power of design. Donghia, known for its furniture, textiles, lighting, and accessories, vacated its SoHo New York facilities while Bergamo, a premier source of textiles from Italy, expanded its operations to join with Donghia in a three-story, 40,000-square-foot space that is so stylish and functional it reinvents what was once an industrial building. Interestingly, the headquarters facilities, including main reception, design studios, private offices, open work areas, boardroom, café and staff support spaces, do not suppress the identity of the wood structure, its high ceilings, industrial windows or wood floors. Instead, the design connects all functions around a long, open circulation spine that is flooded with daylight, warmth and Old World character, integrating sleek modern architecture and traditional interior design—featuring Donghia's own products, of course—with the building's

basic elements. Such adaptations as the conversion of the original loading dock into the main reception and connecting stair have turned the original construction into a memorable workplace and showcase.

Right: Breakout area
Below: Main reception
Bottom left: Open office area
Bottom right: Café
Opposite: Boardroom
Photography: Andrea Brizzi

Conant Architects

Financial Institution
New York, New York

Lack of natural light and a low ceiling saddled with immovable ductwork can make office space seem confining and oppressive, as any prospective tenant immediately senses. But the renovation of a one-floor, 14,400-square-foot office for the client, a major savings bank with 34 branches serving greater New York, reveals how good design can overcome such obstacles. The Manhattan facility, which includes reception, private offices, workstation clusters, resource library, copy room, pantry, restrooms and storage, has been designed by Conant Architects with creative architectural details that open up the existing construction for 48 employees. The successful design begins with a straightforward linear floor plan based on the existing column grid. However, where conventional schemes might blanket the low, dark space with light, Conant Architects introduces such features as light coves with "penetrating" floor-to-ceiling "waterfall" glass sheets in seemingly continuous flow, and linear and accent lighting combined with a black reflective marble tile floor to create a striking main circulation path. There are also a variety of light coves and lighting fixtures that harvest light from a wide range of sources. With so much attention paid to its perceived boundaries, this client's modern, black-and-white space comes off as open, energetic and unexpectedly appealing.

Francis Cauffman

Francis Cauffman LifeCell
Branchburg, New Jersey

How do you reconstruct a facility while its occupants work inside? The complex process is sometimes likened to surgery, an analogy that may seem apt to LifeCell, which functioned throughout the renovation of its two-floor, 140,000-square-foot office and manufacturing

Top left: Reception

Above: Branding wall in central corridor

Right: Communicating stair

Far right: Link space and cafeteria

Photography: Jeffrey Totaro

plant in Branchburg, New Jersey, designed by Francis Cauffman. A major developer and marketer of tissue repair products for use in reconstructive, urogyneco-logic and orthopedic surgical procedures, LifeCell looked to Francis Cauffman to develop the phasing strategies, temporary moves and swing spaces to keep 400 employ-ees working. Equally impor-tant, LifeCell challenged Francis Cauffman to raise the performance level of the facility, initiating discussions, evaluations of existing circu-lation patterns, and studies of how people worked within the existing space. The end result is a new environment providing a main corridor, clear delineation between public, R&D and executive spaces, and a uniform work-place emphasizing openness and sustainability. Informal meeting areas enhance per-formance, communications and collaboration. There is even a dramatic flourish at the main corridor's far end, the "link space" bordering the cafeteria. This large infor-mal meeting area features a two-story space, rich textures, clerestory windows, and a branding wall, an appropri-ately expansive, sunlit and life-affirming "town hall" for a leader in regenerative medicine.

Francis Cauffman

Cole, Schotz, Meisel, Forman & Leonard
Wilmington, Delaware

Making the most of limited real estate, the Wilmington, Delaware office of Cole, Schotz, Meisel, Forman & Leonard recently opened a new, one-floor, 6,500-square-foot facility, designed by Francis Cauffman, that appears spacious and airy while discreetly separating public space from attorney space. The subtlety is not surprising for Cole, Schotz, a prominent law firm founded in 1928, whose 120 attorneys in four offices serve closely-held businesses, individuals and Fortune 500 companies throughout the mid-Atlantic region. Careful placement of key components makes this scheme particularly successful. The conference and reception centers are strategically located to help conceal attorney space from public view while enabling easy access to staff. Perimeter offices are outfitted with glass-panel doors that allow diffused light to penetrate the inner support spaces. Classic modern architecture is finished in rich woods, including Santo rosewood and dark walnut, plus warm neutrals to establish a calm, gracious and assuring ambiance. Adding to the effect is the design's consistency, extending a high level of detailing, along with such materials as the hardwood finishes, honed marble tile, carpet, glass and acoustical and gypsum ceilings, to spaces clients never see.

Above: Office corridor
Right: Conference center
Opposite: Reception
Photography: Francis Cauffman

Francis Cauffman

Fox Rothschild LLP
Philadelphia, Pennsylvania

A four-floor, 104,500-square-foot space for the Philadelphia office of Fox Rothschild may not appear to be a confined space, at least to the casual onlooker. But the need to include reception, private offices, support staff areas, conference center, library, two lunch rooms, two client coffee bars, training rooms and mail and copy rooms to accommodate 359 employees as well as visiting clients makes Fox Rothschild's dynamic, contemporary space, designed by Francis Cauffman, that much more impressive. Resolving complex issues comes naturally to the prominent

Philadelphia-based law firm, founded in 1907, whose 450 attorneys provide a full range of legal services ranging from traditional services (litigation, corporate, labor and employment) to emerging ones (intellectual property and tech and venture finance) to the corporate community in 15 offices coast to coast. However, the design goes to considerable lengths to make the firm's work more effective and enjoyable as well as compact. A connecting stair, for example, links all attorney spaces to reinforce communication and cooperation among the firm's attorneys. Elsewhere, high-density

filing has helped consolidate and condense support staff members, who occupy 120 workstations. Four-person legal administration work zones at the quadrants of each floor promote efficiency and organization, and the application of numerous

Left: Reception
Above left: Conference room
Above right: View from reception to connecting stair
Photography: David Lamb

Francis Cauffman

green design principles promotes sustainability and the well-being of the staff. Green features are ambitious and extensive, comprising low-VOC paints and adhesives, rubber and cork flooring at employee coffee and copy areas, recycled content in ceiling tile, carpet, reception desk and credenza, counter tops, side lites at all perimeter offices, filtered water in lieu of bottled water, CFC-free and Energy Star-rated appliances, FSC-certified wood millwork and furniture, systems furniture manufactured within a 500-mile radius, and a demountable glass system. Visitors may be forgiven for first noticing another admirable feature, however. The interiors, appointed in natural walnut, travertine, clear, frosted and back-painted glass, carpet, rubber and cork flooring, as well as fine, contemporary furnishings and sophisticated lighting, are undeniably as beautiful as they are functional.

Above: Lunchroom

Gensler

Gensler

Noodles & Company
Broomfield, Colorado

Driven to "Nourish & Inspire," Noodles & Company has been the highest-ranking restaurant among the *Inc.* 500 roster of "America's Fastest Growing Private Companies" four years in a row. The youthful enterprise, founded in 1995 in Boulder, Colorado, has become a leader in the fast casual food category—opening over 100 restaurants across the nation in less than 10 years—by serving simple yet satisfying dishes created from natural ingredients in a fresh, comfortable and colorful environment. Its new, one-floor, 23,000-square-foot corporate headquarters, in a Broomfield, Colorado retail strip, has been designed by Gensler to meet ever-growing demands to attract franchisees, showcase the brand, retain talent and provide a workplace embodying the essence of its thriving culture. How do you create an environment to stimulate employee creativity as well as support ongoing operations? Gensler's project team has conceived the headquarters as a village that accommodates many types of activities and occupants. The notion of an open office space organized into a series of neighborhoods connected by intersections, alleys and plazas is not far fetched considering Noodles' diverse workforce, which includes marketing professionals, graphic designers, facility operations managers, salespersons, restaurant designers and in-house culinary experts. Mixing formal and informal uses as the ebb and flow of the workday requires, the workstation neighborhoods are arrayed in grids with conference rooms and lounge areas dispersed like landmarks among them to act as collaboration hubs, and are linked together by the undulating walls of the central corridor that serves as the village's main street, joining the entrance to the full test kitchen and employee café. Not surprisingly, the

Left: Test kitchen

Top: Reception

Above: Workstation neighborhood

Opposite: Library

Photography: Ben Tremper

Gensler

Above right: Break area
Right: Lounge
Far right: Private offices
Opposite top: Wall detail

52

design incorporates stylistic components of Noodles' restaurants, including furniture, lighting, signage and equipment, everywhere. Yet the design also interprets the restaurants' free spirit by taking the approach of "less is best" to forms, materials and colors, minimalizing the carpet, ceiling tile and drywall used, and combining them with such deconstructed and casual elements as oriented strand board, wood timbers and bean bag chairs. (Noodles is not a LEED project, but sustainability is visible in many design aspects, such as the exposed concrete floor, exposed ceiling, low-flow plumbing fixtures and waterless urinals, increased daylight, and bicycle storage area for employees' bikes and company fleet provided for employee use.) Reveling in the "no boundaries" atmosphere of the new space, employees have expressed their praise in such comments as "It just feels like we have more energy here!"

Gensler

Pixar
Emeryville, California

Designing an inspirational and effective workspace for a creative company is particularly challenging when the client is as distinguished as Pixar, an Academy Award-winning computer animation studio with the technical, production and creative capabilities to create groundbreaking animated feature films, merchandise and other related products. The goals were set high from the start, when Gensler was retained to design the gut renovation of an existing structure to create a one-floor, 19,105-square-foot facility for cubicles, conference rooms, private offices, a library and an entrance lobby/café. Pixar was emphatic that the space needed to be of equal quality to its existing headquarters and to contribute to its organically growing campus. The re-designed industrial warehouse would be modern, comfortable and conducive to both maximum employee interaction and the undisturbed flow of the creative process, providing a neutral backdrop for the users while simultaneously reinforcing Pixar's corporate culture through a design aesthetic that celebrated

Top right: Open work area

Above: Central Hall view, rear lounge

Right: View towards conference room from main hallway

Opposite: Community hub and café

Photography: Sharon Risendorph

54

Gensler

the building's industrial origin. Daunting as this challenge would seem to any design firm, the Gensler design team has succeeded in meeting Pixar's expectations. Because the design solution has restored the warehouse shell to its former glory and simultaneously produced an exceptional, state-of-the-art workplace, the space has become known as the "creative factory." Indeed, surrounding the new construction's sleek yet comfortable classic modern furnishings and drywall partitions that stop far short of the ceiling are such reminders of the factory as the walls of industrial window units in steel and translucent glass, and the exposed ceiling of steel trusses, metal roof decking and industrial lighting fixtures, good "bones" to support a young, growing and already quite accomplished organization.

Right: Large conference room view from community hub

Below left: Coffee bar at community hub and entrance

Below right: Coffee bar at coomunity hub/entry to building

H. Hendy Associates

H. Hendy Associates

The Wave Equity Partners
Aliso Viejo, California

Entrepreneurs often spot special opportunities in seemingly ordinary places, and the recent renovation of a two-story, 10,000-square-foot office building and warehouse, in Aliso Viejo, California, by the owner of The Wave Equity Partners, an Orange County Investment and Managment firm, illustrates the impressive possibilities. To fulfill the client's goal of housing his corporate office, foundations office and incubator for start-up businesses in the building, H. Hendy Associates designed a scheme placing the incubator, a temporary facility for start-up businesses to develop until they can afford their own space, on the ground floor, with access to the warehouse, and the corporate office and foundation office upstairs. The cool, highly detailed and largely open workplace of white and gray finishes, accented by horizontals of warm wood, reflects the client's desire for a highly flexible yet seamless contemporary environment evoking an Apple Store. Despite the openness of the environment, the design uses space intensively. For example, since multiple businesses share one conference room, the office incorporates numerous other, smaller meeting areas, and workstations are custom designed to minimize their footprints. From a visionary beginning, the project has arrived at an inspiring destination that has prompted the client to declare, "This office design exceeds our highest expectations."

Left: Private office
Below left: Reception area
Below: Lunchroom
Opposite: Conference room
Photography: Craig Dugan/ Hedrich Blessing

H. Hendy Associates

Green Street Advisors
Newport Beach, California

A firm engaging young Ivy League professionals in independent research, trading and consulting, concentrating on REITs, Green Street Advisors has successfully rebranded itself by relocating from a warren of nondescript suites to a striking and vastly more open, 12,873-square-foot office, in Newport Beach, California, designed by H. Hendy Associates. Green Street intended from the start to create a sophisticated, California beach feel. But there was a catch: Opening up space meant relinquishing private offices in favor of open workstations. Would the firm's high-powered employees accept the change? The new space confronts the question by upgrading the relocation for everyone, combining openness with transparency, group activity areas, and top quality finishes. Accordingly, glass walls enclose private offices to transmit natural light and views deep inside, workstation partitions remain low and finished in wood, and the main conference room includes a banquette. There is built-in bench seating elsewhere to encourage official and impromptu meetings, and the lunchroom is equipped with appliances, stocked with beverages and snacks, and furnished with solid, comfortable furnishings to relieve long hours of demanding work. Assessing the design, Warner Griswold, Green Street's chief operating officer, has commented, "We couldn't be much happier with our space and with Hendy."

Above left: Open workstations
Above right: Lunchroom
Right: Main conference room
Opposite: Reception
Photography: Craig Dugan/ Hedrich Blessing

H. Hendy Associates

Haskell & White
Irvine, California

Design becomes a strategic tool for knowledgeable businesses and their design firms, as visitors can observe at the new, one-floor, 19,000-square-foot office of Haskell & White, in Irvine, California, designed by H. Hendy Associates.

For Haskell & White, one of Orange County's largest, locally owned accounting and consulting firms, moving to this inviting facility combines more space and greater efficiency with "hoteling," a new, alternative office solution, to maximize flexibility.

Everyone knew the previous office's shortcomings. However, while the new layout, located in an Irvine Company high-rise, could easily accommodate growth and alternative/telecommuter officing—especially for the Audit Group, whose

Above: Lunchroom

Above right: Hoteling area

Right: View from reception to corridor

Far right: Reception and main conference room

Opposite top: Main conference room

Photography: Craig Dugan/ Hedrich Blessing

members are present only 20 percent at certain times—Haskell & White questioned the effect on its culture, which openly acknowledges the accomplishments of its teams. H. Hendy's design solution addresses the firm's growing pains as well as its tradition of teamwork through a contemporary space offering a "work anywhere" approach that gives everyone a private office or workstation but anticipates switching to hoteling if necessary. Meanwhile, reminders of the value of teamwork are evident everywhere, including the training room, kitchen and lunchroom, where an exposed ceiling evokes the previous office's balconies so employee accomplishments can still be celebrated "outdoors."

H. Hendy Associates

Overland, Pacific & Cutler, Inc.
Long Beach, California

To manage a 200 percent hold-over cost, a turnkey construction budget of $55/ square foot, a tight construction schedule and a triple-net lease holding it responsible for operating costs, Overland, Pacific & Cutler turned to H. Hendy Associates to design its new, one-floor, 11,000-square-foot office at Douglas Park, a planned business park in Long Beach, California converted from a former McDonnell Douglas aircraft factory. But more was at stake. A real estate consulting company serving public agencies and businesses throughout the nation, Overland, Pacific & Cutler wanted its new premises to exemplify space efficiency, energy conservation, and cost effectiveness within a LEED-like installation quite unlike its conservative former premises and mostly private offices. H. Hendy Associates' solution introduces a contemporary environment of mostly open workstations in an industrial aesthetic that is surprisingly welcoming. Among the innovative touches making the new facility popular with employees and visitors are modified existing workstations, lowering the furniture system's panels and combining them with an up-mounted frameless glass riser to transmit daylight and views, a custom-designed dimmable pendant light fixture, suspended from the exposed ceiling that provides high quality light plus a 33 percent energy savings—and the reinstallation of the firm's iconic fish tank in a harmonious new setting.

Far left: Corridor

Below left: Reception with seating and fish tank

Below right: Office showing open workstation

Photography: Craig Dugan/ Hedrich Blessing

JPC Architects

601 108th Ave NE, Suite 2250 • Bellevue, WA 98004 • 425.641.9200 • 425.637.8200 (F)

www.jpcarchitects.com

JPC Architects   Eastgate Office Commons
Bellevue, Washington

Fifth largest city in Washington with some 120,000 residents, Bellevue is a fast-growing high-tech and retail center in greater Seattle's Eastside district that attracts many software companies. To cater to their needs, Eastgate Office Commons has been designed by JPC Architects as an office park of three seven-story buildings enclosing approximately 22,000 square feet per floor, with an aggregate campus floor area of 600,000 square feet, that balances the requirements for private offices with a distinctive array of public amenity spaces. The design creates a cohesive and highly functional environment that serves over 20 different user groups yet provides a visible sense of community by linking spaces within buildings and distances between buildings through a series of community areas that are interconnected by pathways, sight lines, highly expressive finishes, furnishings, lighting and graphics. Among the key amenities that generate traffic on campus are the central "Great Room," an energetic social gathering space, convenient hub and collaboration areas featuring everything from high bar counter seating and contemporary lounge seating, and a café with four distinct dining venues that could rival a full service restaurant. Diverse as the Eastgate workforce is, tenants regularly declare that they are delighted with its distinctive setting.

Above left: Hub
Above: Corporate dining
Left: Reception and waiting area
Opposite: Great Room
Photography: Benjamin Benschneider

JPC Architects

Metzler North America Corporation
Seattle, Washington

Clockwise from top: Semi-private office, lunchroom, board-room, detail between offices, reception

Photography: Benjamin Benschneider

Metzler North America Corporation is a young boutique real estate investment bank, founded in 1976. Its parent, Bankhaus Metzler, is Germany's oldest privately-held investment bank, established in 1674. The bank asked JPC Architects to design its full-floor, 11,040-square-foot Seattle headquarters to reflect both progressive thinking and timeless stability. The cohesiveness in the completed space testifies to the cooperation between architect and client as well as the creativity of the design team. To convey stability in the interior architecture, the designers took full advantage of the fact that the floor had a unique sloped degree cross-sectional challenge with an expressed curtain wall and structural rhythm. This rhythm created an inherent vocabulary of repetition throught the existing floor which the designers chose to 'play-up' as an aesthetic. The client wanted to create individual work spaces that felt like an office, yet open and approachable. The demising walls that separate each office received an insertion of glass at the window to allow the drama of the slanted curtain wall to read as a continuum. This design gesture provides a sense of visual connectivity to a larger team culture while still maintaining a sense of personal space.

JPC Architects

Lytle Enterprises
Bellevue, Washington

Above left: Entry and reception
Above: Reception
Below left: Executive office

Opposite: Boardroom
Photography: Benjamin Benschneider

Charles and Karen Lytle founded Lytle Enterprises, a leading, privately held builder of quality senior housing since 1976. Three decades later, Lytle Enterprises' new 3,700-square-foot, seven-person executive office in Bellevue, Washington, projects the comfortable, professional and elegant image befitting one of America's leading senior housing developers. Designed by JPC Architects, the award-winning facility includes reception area, private offices, conference rooms, break room and support space, providing an exceptional workplace and gallery for the client's

art collection. The scheme reflects creative planning. To provide the desired "refined contemporary" ambience and abundant daylight, the design establishes a feeling of infinite space with frameless, floor-to-ceiling glass walls and doors for perimeter offices and conference rooms. The indirect cove lighting enhances the interior walls' organic shape. Rich, warm carpeting and upholstery fabrics enhance the elegance of the space. The art collection is accommodated by an undulating sculptural wall linking reception to the private offices. Observes Karen Lytle, "We are just as

thrilled every day we come into the office as the first day we moved in."

JPC Architects

Merriman Berkman Next
Seattle, Washington

Merriman Berkman Next, a Seattle-based money management firm formed by the merger of Merriman Capital Management, a financial planning firm, with Berkman Purdy and Lindstrom, an accounting firm, recently completed a full-floor, 18,000-square-foot office for 98 employees that suggests that the firm's principals and associates are forward-thinking and creative finance professionals. The contemporary facility, designed by JPC Architects, accomplishes this feat by combining open areas with glazed enclosures, and enriching the entire facility with multiple-height ceilings with the furniture in lively colors, patterns and textures. Despite a 50/50 ratio of private offices to open workstations, the space is filled with light due to extensive use of glass in the demountable wall system. The design directs visitors along a carefully choreographed "client path" using walls, lighting and artwork to help them navigate among the private offices, conference rooms, teaming rooms and break area.

Top left: Teaming room
Top right: Reception
Above: Conference room
Photography: Benjamin Benschneider

Kishimoto Gordon Dalaya PC

Kishimoto Gordon Dalaya PC

The Tower Companies
Rockville, Maryland

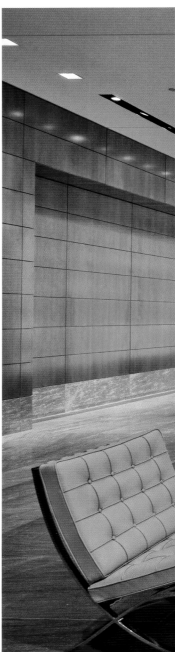

It's rare that a business commits itself to creating the healthiest workplace possible and a LEED Platinum-certified facility, representing the highest level of sustainability. However, the new, one-floor, 21,000-square-foot headquarters of The Tower Companies, a Rockville, Maryland-based real estate developer of environmentally conscious buildings and communities, has met these goals, along with promoting company core values and gaining a competitive advantage. The award-winning space and base building housing it, both designed by Kishimoto Gordon Dalaya, offer Tower an elegant and sophisticated contemporary environment for private offices, open workstations, executive conference facilities, fitness center, café and meditation room, all arranged around a large, open public area serving reception and conferencing. Architect and client worked closely together to assure that the space would balance openness with privacy and conform to Vedic architectural principles in embracing sustainability. Consequently, the needs of the family-owned business and 56 headquarters employees are reflected in such details as the FSC-certified pear wood wall panels, doors, millwork and furniture, ample daylight and outdoor views, handsome new custom and reconditioned furniture, advanced building systems, and energy efficient lighting, which exceeds code requirements for power density by 27 percent. This is an outstanding workplace, and employees proudly acknowledge it.

Right: Reception

Below: Building lobby

Opposite left: Conference room

Opposite upper right: Private offices and indoor plantings

Opposite lower right: Perimeter offices and open workstations

Photography: Ron Blunt

Kishimoto Gordon Dalaya PC

Delucchi +
Washington, D.C.

Real estate marketing firm Delucchi + knew exactly what it wanted for its new, one-floor, 4,944-square-foot office in downtown Washington: a vibrant, open environment with daylight, views and environmentally sustainable design. But there were two additional requirements that could have jeopardized everything: a short timeframe and limited budget. Fortunately, Kishimoto Gordon Dalaya was prepared for this exacting assignment, taking Delucchi + from first meeting to move-in in just five months, staying within budget and winning LEED Silver certification for the design. The floor plan plays a critical role in the solution, because employees in private offices along the perimeter and open work areas, interactive lunch/lounge and conference room in the center find interaction is both convenient and inviting. In addition, the branded interior provides a lively and expansive composition of bright colors and patterns, exposed concrete floors, office furniture made from recycled materials, Green Guard-certified carpet and other green materials and furnishings, and energy efficient lighting monitored by occupancy sensors, producing a workplace where health shares equal prominence with function and aesthetics. Besides, the 35 employees genuinely enjoy their facility as a place where good indoor air is matched by amenities such as Guitar Hero in the lunch/lounge's "playroom."

Lower left: Open workstations
Below: Lunch/lounge
Opposite upper left: Corridor
Opposite upper right: Reception
Photography: Jeff Wolfram

76

Kishimoto Gordon Dalaya PC

Kishimoto Gordon Dalaya PC
Rosslyn, Virginia

Setting objectives as ambitious as those of its clients, Kishimoto Gordon Dalaya, an architecture, interior design and planning firm in Rossyln, Virginia, a suburb of Washington, D.C., has given clients a masterful demonstration of how creative design, technical expertise and comprehensive project management can multiply the impact of a short timeframe and limited budget. The award-winning, one-floor, 9,300-square-foot office that the firm has designed for its 30 employees simultaneously respects the timeframe and budget, achieves LEED Gold certification, and provides an effective work environment where openness, flexibility and collaboration easily coexist with privacy, storage capacity and a dynamic, contemporary aesthetic. Within the mostly open environment, which comprises a studio, private offices, conference rooms, resource library, plotter room, model shop, kitchen and pantry, space remains open in perception if not reality through minimal use of partitions, an exposed ceiling, glass demising walls and doors that enclose conference rooms yet transmit daylight and views, a bold color scheme of black and white accented by marble and composite zebra wood, a modern, open office furniture system with clean lines and elegant details, and unobtrusive, energy conserving lighting. In fact, everything consistently confirms why the corporate and institutional worlds need professional design.

Top left: Studio

Top right: Entry hall

Left: Conference rooms

Above: Breakout area

Photography: Jeff Wolfram

Kishimoto Gordon Dalaya PC

Winkler Family Trust
Alexandria, Virginia

Old Town Alexandria is an historic jewel of northern Virginia, just minutes south of Washington, where Colonial-era architecture and new construction honoring the period combine to preserve one of the region's most charming communities. So when the Winkler Family Trust retained Kishimoto Gordon Dalaya to design its one-floor, 5,000-square-foot headquarters in an existing Old Town building, the goal was to insert a modern office space inside a structure saddled with antiquated construction methods and building systems. The cool, high-technology look of the renovated space discloses little about the formidable problems it resolves. To overcome such constraints as low ceiling heights and limitations on plumbing and HVAC installations, the design team made creative use of space, furniture and finishes to emphasize openness and elevation as much as possible. Such design elements as an exposed ceiling, metal and glass partitions with integral acoustic panels, a bold color scheme contrasting bright whites and deep chocolates with metal and glass, direct/indirect lighting and such art pieces as a custom motorcycle and vintage signage are subtly combined to give the facility the form and function it needs. As a result, the open reception area with adjacent lounge, perimeter offices, conference room, administrative assistant stations and office support areas are equally at home in Old Town and the modern world.

Above: Entry reception
Below left: Conference room
Below: Lounge
Photography: Jeff Wolfram

Mancini·Duffy

39 West 13th Street • New York, NY 10011 • 212.938.1260 • 212.938.1267 (F)
www.manciniduffy.com

Mancini·Duffy

Fitzpatrick, Cella, Harper & Scinto
New York, New York

Renovate in place or relocate? Confronting an office at midtown Manhattan's Rockefeller Center that no longer met its needs, the New York headquarters of Fitzpatrick, Cella, Harper & Scinto recently engaged Mancini·Duffy to evaluate its real estate options. Founded in 1971 by six partners to provide top quality legal services in intellectual property, Fitzpatrick, Cella has become one of America's premier intellectual property law firms, with 175 attorneys in New York, Washington, D.C. and Costa Mesa, California. Mancini·Duffy developed a space program for the New York office to conduct test fits of the existing premises and six alternatives before the attorneys chose an all-new, three-floor, 130,000-square-foot space in 1290 Avenue of the Americas. Marking the first time that Fitzpatrick, Cella's New York office has been developed expressly for itself, the new, contemporary facility reflects the expanded practice and diverse scientific and industry backgrounds of its personnel with its conferencing center, private offices, open workstations, multi-purpose training room, staff pantry with outdoor terrace, and advanced technology and video conferencing. Another sign of the times is the standardization of office sizes and furniture components, anticipating Fitzpatrick, Cella's need for greater flexibility and lower reconfiguration costs in the inevitable inter-office moves to come.

Opposite top left: Reception

Opposite top right: Private offices and workstations

Right: Lobby and interior stair

Below: Conference room and pre-function area

Photography: Eric Laignel

Mancini·Duffy

Citi Field
Flushing, New York

One of New York's most anticipated new buildings in 2009 was Citi Field, the 42,500-seat New York Mets ballpark. Besides giving the Mets a modern sports venue, Citi Field houses a sleek new Mets front office, a two-floor, 60,000-square-foot facility designed by Mancini·Duffy.

The contemporary space features a dynamic series of folded, floating and luminous planes enriched by such contrasting materials as wood, metal and glass, colors that display the Mets' blue and orange alongside natural hues, and a range of textures. Besides reflecting the Major

League Baseball team's heritage, the design creates a memorable workplace. On the fourth floor, 14-foot ceilings, office fronts of frosted glass and wood panels, clerestory windows, stainless steel columns, floating ceiling planes and art produce appropriate

settings for the reception area, executive suite, boardroom, conference areas and private offices, many with dramatic views of the ballpark interior. On the third floor, the sales and marketing group, gym and employee lunchroom are characterized by metal mesh café chairs,

pin-striped carpet and grass-green walls. Simpler yet equally compelling, the street-level lobby greets visitors with a long, L-shaped luminous desk, classic modern lounge furnishings—and a spectacular, 105-inch flat-screen LCD TV showcasing the Amazins' on-field play.

Top: Boardroom

Left: Pre-function area outside boardroom

Right: Lobby

Photography: Eric Laignel

Mancini·Duffy

Morrison & Foerster
Washington, D.C.

Right: Conference room

Far right: Corridor in conference center

Below: Interior staircase and feature wall

Photography: Mark Ballogg Photography

Frequently, at the heart of today's law office is a modern conference center where attorneys and clients conduct major transactions backed by an array of support services. Such is the case in the 134,000-square-foot renovation and expansion of global law firm Morrison & Foerster's Washington, D.C. office, designed by Mancini·Duffy. The new scheme lets the law firm remain in 2000 Pennsylvania Avenue, the building it has occupied for 20 years, for at least 15 more years while upgrading the facilities to the same standards of innovation and excellence of its high-profile practice groups. Besides connecting, unifying and modernizing the space, the new design opens a state-of-the-art conference center that doubles as a venue for interaction among practice area leaders. Twenty conference rooms and several flexible breakout spaces form the center's nucleus, which occupies the middle of the building and is shared among the four floors to link the office vertically as well as east-to-west on the building's elongated floorplate. The center shares the spotlight, however, with a four-story, stone-and-glass feature wall that serves as a background for the interior staircase. Comprising split-face Jerusalem limestone tiles in a vertical running bond pattern, the wall is simply too beautiful to ignore.

Mancini·Duffy

Council on Foreign Relations
Washington, D.C.

Changing from leasing to owning has opened fresh opportunities for the not-for-profit Council on Foreign Relations at its new, award-winning Washington office at 1777 F Street, designed by Mancini·Duffy. With 10 floors totaling 61,450 square feet near the White House, the building represented an attractive investment as well as ample space for CFR's staff and a new conference center. The LEED Gold renovation unifies an historic 1870s-era townhouse, replica townhouse and 1980s-era office building so they function as a single unit inside and out. Taking cues from the historic townhouse, the design team has reclad the buildings to harmonize palette and proportion and increase sustainability. Inside, the three contiguous parts now feel like one building,

and their upgraded workplace environment, based on sound existing structure and MEP systems and versatile floorplates, promotes energy conservation, indoor air quality and natural light. As for the 350-seat conference center, equipped with skyfold partitions, plasma screens, broadcast studio, audio editing studio and AV control room, it has quickly become the flourishing Washington venue long sought by CFR, an independent, nonpartisan think tank and membership organization founded in 1921 to promote understanding of U.S. foreign policy and America's role in the world.

Above right: Stair tower
Right: Typical office floor
Below: Conference center
Photography: Mark Ballogg Photography

Mancini·Duffy

BT Americas
New York, New York

One plus one can equal one—at least when an organization consolidates offices. To help BT Americas—which provides networked IT services, including high performance networking, convergence & collaboration, security, contact center and enterprise mobility solution—determine the best strategy for unifying five New York-area offices, Mancini·Duffy developed test fits detailing the implications

of various scenarios. Once BT Americas chose to relocate and consolidate on floors 45 and 46 of the New York Times Building, the 50-story office tower designed by Renzo Piano and completed in 2007, Mancini·Duffy turned to a very different challenge. Since the design team's mandate was to design the two-level, 63,000-square-foot facility to align with the British parent company's standards, BT

Americas now has a unique office that is highly collaborative and non-hierarchical—with no private offices at all. Instead, the space features 400 open desks that occupy the building perimeter, letting daylight and views be shared by all, teaming areas that are distributed throughout the floor, encouraging frequent and impromptu collaboration, and glass-walled conference rooms that hug

the building core, balancing privacy with connectivity. Other highlights of this distinctive, forward-looking environment include the European-style "benching" system for workstations, building products with recycled content, the connecting stair for healthier circulation, and the

welcoming café, where brown-bagging lunch has never seemed so stylish.

Top: Entry and reception
Above: Reception seating
Left: Meeting area
Photography: Eric Laignel

Margulies Perruzzi Architects

Margulies Perruzzi Architects

Sapient World Headquarters
Boston, Massachusetts

Working in a dynamic and changing world much as its customers do, Sapient, one of the world's largest interactive advertising agencies, has developed a new, one-floor, 36,000-square-foot headquarters, in Boston, that exemplifies today's interactive workplace. The contemporary facility, designed by Margulies Perruzzi Architects, places 200 employees in an environment where the reception, open and private offices, conference and meeting rooms, breakout rooms, design center, production space, café and wellness room range from compact individual accommodations (mobile workstations provide 185 square feet per person) to spacious public areas. Its open plan configuration simultaneously supports operating groups within well-defined "neighborhoods," comprising color-coded clusters of workstations and meeting spaces, and unites the staff through a corridor that doubles as a public forum, featuring carpet in Sapient's orange color and video screens displaying the company's work, as it directs employees and clients from the entrance to the centrally located conference rooms and café. Fitted with efficient, flexible furnishings, the facility enjoys generous daylight and views because private offices occupy the interior, keeping peripheral areas unobstructed, while such decorative elements as the lobby mural, designed by a staff graphic designer, and photos and images contributed by employees impart the human touch even the cyberworld appreciates.

Right: Neighborhood

Lower right: Lobby mural

Lower far right: Mobile workstations

Bottom right: Café

Below: Main lobby

Photography: Warren Patterson

Margulies Perruzzi Architects

Global Healthcare Products Company
Mansfield, Massachusetts

The opening of a two-floor, 80,000-square-foot headquarters could not be more appropriate for a newly branded $10 billion global healthcare products company in Mansfield, Massachusetts, a Boston suburb. Designed by Margulies Perruzzi Architects, the construction converts a nondescript light manufacturing facility into an effective, world-class office building. Of course, the development of a corporate headquarters with a formal entry, lobby/reception, open and private offices, conference rooms, multi-media conference rooms, gallery space, cafeteria and locker rooms required both architectural and engineering modifications. Large expanses of glass were incorporated in the exterior walls, for example, to capture natural light and views, using a "saw tooth" configuration of perimeter private offices with glass fronts to extend these amenities deep indoors. New building MEP systems were installed to provide state-of-the-art performance. The narrow existing entry corridor was replaced by a semi-circular entry rotunda. Equally important, an inviting, open interior was created featuring a neutral color scheme with bright accents for wayfinding and orientation, a material palette of cherry wood, aluminum, granite, glass, carpet and other quality materials, and "task and team"-style office furniture suited to both individual and group activities, giving 600 headquarters employees a healthy start in their new workplace.

Top right: Cafeteria

Top left: Casual meeting area and conference rooms

Upper left: Multi-media conference room

Left: Gallery space

Opposite: Lobby and reception

Photography: Warren Patterson

Margulies Perruzzi Architects

Margulies Perruzzi Architects
Boston, Massachusetts

Windowless and vacant for years, a former storage space on the fourth floor of the Boston Children's Museum has been revived by Margulies Perruzzi Architects, which recently designed a lively, 13,000-square-foot office for its own 50 employees to fill the void. Located directly above active exhibit space, the new facility occupies a part of the Museum's brick-and-timber wharf building that functioned as a wool processing warehouse in 1888. The installation of a reception area, open and private offices, conference and meeting rooms, copy room, and café inevitably required alterations, adding several large windows, installing a roof deck, and soundproofing the floor to block sounds from below. Yet the new interior, contrasting brick walls and oak beams with cool modern finishes accented by an intensely bright blue color, is about more than aesthetics. Developed to receive LEED Silver certification through such sustainable provisions as Energy Star-rated equipment, reused furniture, and locally sourced and low-VOC-emitting materials, the new interior's glass enclosed private offices and conference rooms, centrally located meeting and conference rooms, and low workstation partitions simultaneously diffuse daylight and views and encourage employee interaction. It's an appealing invitation to appraise the capabilities of a firm celebrating its 20th year in business.

Right: Reception

Far right: Private and open offices

Below: Lobby and main conference room

Opposite top: Open office workstations and movable walls

Photography: Warren Patterson

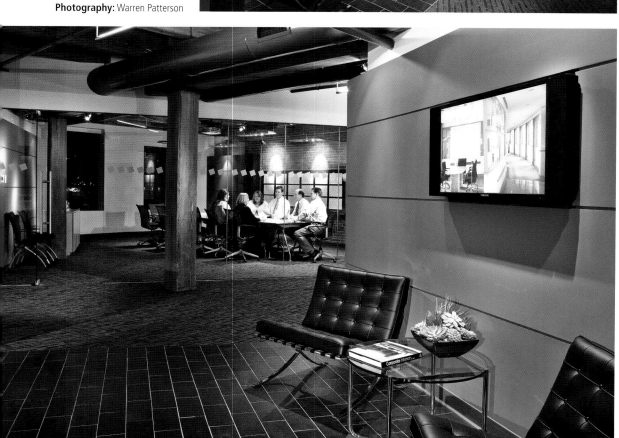

Margulies Perruzzi Architects

Worldwide Financial Services Company
Portsmouth, New Hampshire

A 110,000-square-foot floor is commonplace in manufacturing. However, the adaptation of 25,000 square feet in a single-story office building attached to 85,000 square feet of high-bay manufacturing space in Portsmouth, New Hampshire to serve as a call center and conference/training facility for 450 employees of a worldwide financial services company was not business as usual. The successful conversion, designed by Margulies Perruzzi Architects, employs multiple strategies to turn the open, high-ceiling structure with little natural light into office space. To break up the floor area, the design established zone one, in the office building, for reception, conference, cafeteria and fitness facilities, and zone two, in the manufacturing facility, for a call center bisected by a primary corridor containing copy room, conference rooms and support spaces. To capture daylight and views, large windows were inserted into the exterior walls. And to scale down the high-bay elevation, the facility incorporated a raised floor, equipped with underfloor HVAC system, as well as a stepped ceiling that lowers its height as it recedes from the perimeter. Equally important, interiors were appointed in modern furnishings as comfortable and colorful as they are functional, marking the building's transition from machinery to people as its focus.

Top right: Reception and main lobby
Upper right: Primary corridor
Lower right: Call center
Below: Casual meeting space
Photography: Warren Patterson

MKDA

MKDA

Rockefeller Philanthropy Advisors
New York, New York

Rockefeller Philanthropy Advisors, one of the world's largest philanthropy services with offices in New York, Los Angeles and San Francisco and a network of affiliates and partner organizations worldwide, has opened a new, three-floor, 17,000-square-foot New York office where 61 employees help donors in the United States and abroad create thoughtful, effective philanthropy. Honoring its unique global mission, the organization worked closely with MKDA to develop a facility to maximize the resources of the small boutique building it occupies, delivering the impact normally found only in much larger facilities. Its classic, modern environment, including reception area, private offices, open workstations, conferencing facilities, and lunch room/breakout room, incorporates numerous features inspired by the latest sustainable design practices. To use space and building materials efficiently, for example, the design conscientiously exploits the building's floorplate, existing construction and even 35 burl wood doors salvaged from the previous tenant's installation, which are seamlessly integrated in the new walls along with new cherry wood paneling. It also addresses other environmental concerns through sustainable building materials, ergonomic furnishings and user-friendly, high-efficiency lighting. As a result, Rockefeller Philanthropy Advisors has achieved a distinguished environment that is life sustaining as well as productive.

Upper right: Lunch room/breakout room

Right: Reception

Below: Conference room

Opposite top center and right: Private office, open workstation

Photography: Tom Sibley

MKDA

MKDA
New York, New York

As an accomplished New York-based design firm, founded in 1959 and specializing in commercial interiors and design, MKDA has opened the doors to a new, one-floor, 10,000-square-foot office for its 35 employees that confirms what every successful design professional must know: a design firm's own premises functions simultaneously as a workplace for personnel and a showroom for clients. This is why the facility, which includes a studio, private offices, conference rooms, library, workroom and lunchroom, employs an open studio layout, offering a wide range of formal and informal spaces for client interaction as well as employee collaboration. The clean, modern and environmentally sensitive setting, comprised of neutral gray, white and wood tones with red accent, and designed with zebra wood veneer, drywall, glass, modern furnishings, carpet, carpet tile, and high-efficiency lighting with daylight harvesting, is very open. In fact, given the low workstation partitions, few doors even for private offices, and numerous teaming areas, staff members were initially hesitant about the high degree of exposure. However, everyone has happily embraced the new scheme, which many a contemporary employer with a young, bright and energetic work force could easily put to good use in an instant.

Above: Principal's office

Left: Entrance and reception

Right: Conference room

Lower right: Small conference room

Bottom right: Studio

Photography: Steve Amiaga

MKDA

CVC Capital Partners
New York, New York

Clockwise from top left:
Open workstations, conference room with company logo on glass, corridor, reception, executive office, elevator lobby

Photography: Tom Sibley

102

Because the look had to be as correct as the function, CVC Capital Partners engaged MKDA early in the leasing phase to see how this leading international private equity and investment advisory firm, headquartered in Luxembourg with offices across Europe, Asia and the United States, would be perceived in its chosen midtown Manhattan space at 712 Fifth Avenue. The one floor, 10,000-square-foot space was carefully studied before the existing interior was demolished. Then, an elegant new traditional office suite for 20 employees emerged from the raw space to establish CVC's corporate presence. Though the office is meticulously detailed to re-inforce the company's global brand, it is also deliberately configured to host meetings with investors. The critical public zone features a large reception area surrounded by multiple conference rooms, and is served by the private zone's private offices, open workstations, pantry and support areas. Visitors will find a finely tailored corporate environment awaits them, appointed in limestone floors, Sapele mahogany, woven carpet, fabric wall-covering, leather upholstery, and glass sandblasted with the CVC logo, along with custom-made furniture and millwork and other modern furnishings, to ensure that CVC's New York office is the equal of its European counterparts.

MKDA

GE Monogram Design Center
New York, New York

Food arouses passion in New York, where millions representing virtually every racial, ethnic and national origin savor the world's great cuisines. Their devotion is evident in the new, one-floor, 8,000-square-foot GE Monogram Design Center, a high-end kitchen appliance showroom in midtown Manhattan. Open to kitchen designers, architects, contract remodelers and the public, the Center has been designed by MKDA as a luxurious, residential-style showroom with three different kitchens and a wine-themed lounge supported by reception, office and conference room. Visitors experience the facility at multiple levels, learning the story of the company and its products at the same time they examine the products. Every detail embodies a story, in effect, beginning with the New York City map on the terrazzo floor, which uses Broadway to guide visitors. Quoting New York's architectural styles and building materials, the stylish and inviting environment feels intriguingly familiar and fresh. Its vocabulary of wood, terrazzo, carpet, leather, fabrics, brick, stone, composites and ceramic and glass tile evokes the good life to dwellers of apartments, townhouses and detached homes alike. Merrill Grant, general manager of the GE Monogram brand, declares, "When you get off the elevator, it pulls you right in."

Above: Ovens and conference room

Right in descending order: Refrigerator wall, entry and recepetion, lounge and wine vault, pro kitchen

Photography: Power Creative

M Moser Associates

257 Park Avenue South, Suite 1101 • New York, NY 10010 • 212.227.0722 • 212.227.0723 (F)

14/F North Somerset House, Taikoo Place, 979 King's Road • Quarry Bay, Hong Kong • 852.2806.1373 • 852.2806.1403 (F)

Beijing • Delhi • Guangzhou • Hong Kong • Kuala Lumpur • London • New York • Shanghai • Shenzhen • Singapore • Taipei

www.mmoser.com

M Moser Associates

Nokia
BDA Site
Beijing, China

A need to consolidate operations into a single site drove the creation of Nokia's new headquarters campus in Beijing—and led to a building of truly radical character. The site's remoteness from the city center meant that gaining end-user acceptance was a major project challenge. In response, M Moser Associates designers engaged with the client's management and 2300 local staff to reveal objectives and needs. The result was a six-story structure conceived literally from the inside-out to offer a unique new "work-life experience." Notably, almost half of the building's 775000 sq-ft floor area is devoted to various amenities arrayed around a central 'main street' atrium. As well as enjoying many dining and leisure options, staff can do their grocery shopping, visit the wellness center, and take care of other everyday personal activities without leaving the site. Workspaces are open-plan to foster easy communication and collaboration. To ensure that the environment is healthy as well as functional, the design incorporates abundant natural lighting, a high-quality air system, sustainable materials, and comfortable Scandinavian-style furnishings. The award-winning effort by designer and client has been successful from the start. With just 0.1 percent turnover resulting from the relocation, Nokia's staff has overwhelmingly bought into their new workplace.

Above left: Work spaces are largely open-plan volumes, with break-out areas established along circulation paths

Above: Office circulation path

Below left: Meeting rooms

Below: One of various dining locations along "Main Street"

Opposite: "Town Center" in open atrium

Photography: Vitus Lau

M Moser Associates

Birmingham Post & Mail
Birmingham, United Kingdom

News organizations thrive on access to information, reporting and writing skills, and collaboration among colleagues, and these factors have powerfully shaped the new, one-floor, 53000 sq-ft office for 550 employees of the *Birmingham Post & Mail,* in Birmingham, United Kingdom. The design by M Moser Associates supports individual and teamwork through such spaces as the boardroom, big enough to hold up to 120 people, the editorial hub, where all 20 editors are situated, and the meeting rooms and breakout areas that surround the hub. These are functional spaces, in keeping with the no-nonsense tradition of news-papers, which is reflected in their use of glazed partitions, steel columns, galvanized ceilings, and laminated doors. But the lighting is good, the contemporary furniture is ergonomic, and the colour scheme introduces splashes of brightness to energize the essentially neutral palette. For employees in a facility busy on a 24/7 basis, having high-performance offices supported by breakout areas, restaurant, showers and day care greatly improves the ability to perform through hours of typically charged and stressful activity. Originally published as the *Daily Post* in 1857, the *Birmingham Post & Mail* now has an appropriate home for documenting its third century of breaking news.

Below: Breakout lounge

Opposite, clockwise from top left: Managers' offices, reception area, breakout spaces in front of presentation/board rooms, team rooms, café

Photography: Simon Triggwell

M Moser Associates

Principal Global Investors, LLC
New York, New York

Asset management services are global products delivered locally whenever clients visit their branch offices. For this reason, the new, one-floor, 19800 sq-ft New York office for 49 employees of Des Moines, Iowa-based Principal Global Investors consciously provides the kind of "pleasant journey" expected by residents of the nation's financial center. The bold, contemporary space, designed by M Moser Associates, simultaneously represents a sophisticated, high-end interior on a stringent budget, a LEED-certified environment that conserves water, energy and electric lighting, and an effortless wayfinding experience that guides visitors along the corridor through visual cues. To create an aesthetically pleasing, confident and inspiring setting, the design incorporates such materials and furnishings as Argentinian cowhide wall and floor coverings, custom leather banquettes, stone-clad reception desks, modern furniture, and decorative glass partitions connected with dark mahogany panels that display small statues and ancient icons from cultures worldwide. Reinforcing this glossy image are such highly functional interiors as reception, offices, meeting rooms, pantry and visitors' desks, all supported by low-flow water fixtures, energy-efficient light fixtures, daylight sensors, and energy-efficient HVAC units. Praising the project's beauty, responsibility and efficiency, Jim McCaughan, president of Principal Global Investors, declares, "We are very excited about our new space."

Left: Employee entry seen from elevator lobby

Below: Reception

Opposite, clockwise from top: Meeting room, private office, open workstations, pantry

Photography: Chris Goodney

M Moser Associates

Ogilvy & Mather
Guangzhou, Guangdong, China

Legendary advertising agency Ogilvy & Mather has developed a three-level (ground floor, mezzanine, first floor), 10807 sq-ft office that turns a potentially difficult relocation into a workplace staff and clients truly enjoy. Located in a newly developed arts and culture district one hour from the center of Guangzhou, the design took inspiration from a theme dubbed "A Carnival of Ideas." Ogilvy and M Moser Associates, the office's designer, appropriately incorporated amusement park elements with exaggerated branding to encourage employees to explore new ideas and deliver great results. To organize functions, the space is anchored by the angled and illuminated red staircase at the center, connecting the lower marketing level to the upper creative level and simultaneously defining the boundary between client meeting/breakout spaces at the front, and offices, pantry, library and shower at the back. Of course, along with the stair, reception area carousel, wrap-around windows, and boardroom merry-go-round horse concealing A/V equipment, there are also modern, functional furnishings to support everyday activities. That's why Michael Lee, COO of Ogilvy Shanghai & Southern China, reports, "Our people simply love it here. Also, our clients like this space so much, some of them specifically request that meetings take place here rather than in their own offices!"

Below left: Breakout space outside boardroom
Below right in descending order: Reception, stair, mezzanine
Photography: Virgile Simon Bertrand

Mojo·Stumer Associates

Mojo·Stumer Associates

Prentice Capital Management
New York, New York

A New York-based money management organization with over $1 billion under management, Prentice Capital Management is young, forward-looking and willing to roll up its sleeves as an active investor. What kind of work environment would best suit its 40 employees? The optimum solution turns out to be a one-story, 17,000-square-foot facility, designed by Mojo•Stumer Associates, that is corporate in tone, yet reflects Prentice's lively and modern style. The office configuration follows standard business layouts, featuring private offices and conference rooms on the perimeter, open plan workstations in the interior, and a reception area, lunchroom and kitchen. However, there are also a gym, recreation area and lounge where employees can balance the demands of work. The look of the office recognizes the need for balance as well. Although it began as an exercise in minimalism, it became a more nuanced image with the development of complex architectural forms, the selection of soft,

monochromatic earth tones, timeless materials like wood, stone, stainless steel and black-painted metal, and stylish contemporary furnishings, and the installation of sophisticated lighting for Prentice's superb photography collection.

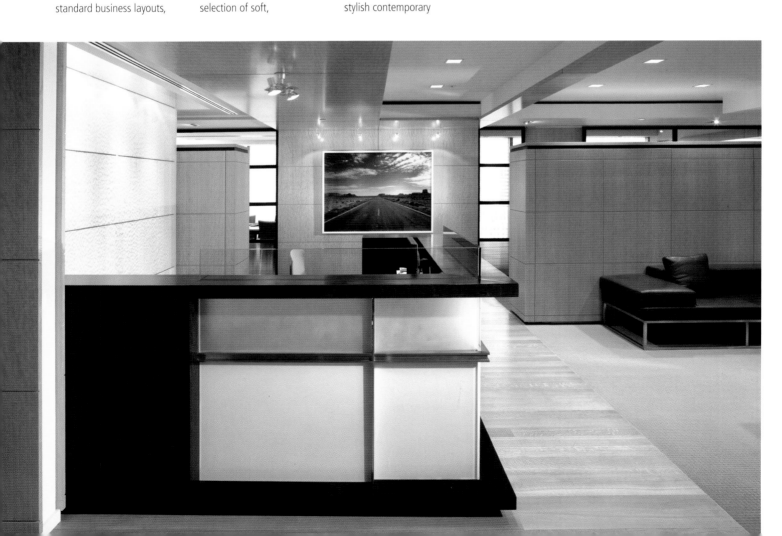

Mojo·Stumer Associates

We're Group
Jericho, New York

Sooner or later, the shoe-maker's children get their shoes. For We're Group, a Jericho, New York-based merchant builder that designs, builds, owns and operates office properties, its new headquarters summarizes over 50 years and three generations of family ownership. Accordingly, the facility's impressive, 8,000-square-foot executive section, designed by Mojo•Stumer Associates, achieves efficiency and grace through economy and taste. Every space, from private offices, conference rooms and reception to file storage, feels spacious and elegant. The reception area, for example, flows into the circulation spine to extend its area, while glass walls give private offices and conference rooms privacy with openness. We're Group loves the design, genuine praise from a developer of 10 million square feet of space.

Mojo·Stumer Associates

Mojo•Stumer Associates
Greenvale, New York

The moment you enter the new, one-level, 6,000-square-foot office, designed by Mojo•Stumer Associates in Greenvale, New York to house its own 30-member staff, you sense this is not your average architecture studio. An architect usually covers the walls with photographs and renderings of projects to complement scale models scattered across the floor. Here, you won't find images on any wall. The clean, elegant and meticulously detailed walls, ceilings and floors create a spacious, subtly illuminated and clearly defined environment that expresses the firm's mission, "Improving the quality of our clients' lives through better and more creative architecture." The construction, consisting of slate, cold-rolled steel and other metals, etched glass, lacquer, ash and maple, is impressive despite the rigorous tests of time, budget and function they have passed to provide a reception area, conference room, two studios (one for architecture, one for interior design), library, private offices and file space. Why shouldn't the award-winning work of a firm founded in 1980 by Thomas Mojo, AIA and Mark Stumer, AIA, to create handsome and practical design for residential, office, leisure and retail clients, be enjoyed by those who create it? For the Mojo•Stumer staff, the new facility literally brings good design home.

Mojo·Stumer Associates

I-Park Lobby
Lake Success, New York

Few factories deserve footnotes in history, but the I-Park Complex, a one million-square-foot industrial campus in Lake Success, New York, does. As the home of Sperry Gyroscope, a navigational equipment manufacturer, during World War II, the campus served as the temporary headquarters of the United Nations in the late 1940s. The recent conversion of a 3,000-square-foot lobby by Mojo•Stumer Associates contrasts the building's original flavor with a contemporary design in stainless steel, wood, terrazzo and glass, featuring a new reception desk, industrial finishes and a new column capital detail that illuminates the existing ceiling—and the building's distinguished past.

Mojo·Stumer Associates

Community National Bank
Woodbury, New York

While nobody expects today's banking halls to resemble the Neoclassical temples of yesteryear, banking customers understandably still favor traditional signs of security and trust wherever they deposit their money. The desire to balance lively modern design concepts with timeless banking themes has produced an exceptionally attractive space at Community National Bank's new, one-floor, 3,800-square-foot retail store in Woodbury, New York, designed by Mojo•Stumer Associates. Housing the third branch of an institution founded in 2005 as a full service commercial bank offering a wide array of deposit and loan products, the Woodbury space is a compact design comprising a tellers' counter, open work areas, conference room and manager's office. The facility feels larger than it is because the design skillfully manipulates its boundaries through multiple wall and ceiling planes. No expanse of wall runs long before being interrupted by another located closer or further from the center of the space, for example, while wall surfaces keep changing from wood to glass or drywall, the latter painted white or the bank's signature blue. Overhead, soffits and coffers tease the eye by altering the ceiling's height. A bank promising customers highly personalized service should offer many points of view, after all.

118

Mojo·Stumer Associates

Barley Ziecheck Medical Offices
New York, New York

Hospitals are increasingly taking cues from hotel and residential design to make their environments more patient-centered, user-friendly and inviting. So it's not surprising that doctors' offices are following suit. At the new, one-floor, 3,500-square-foot Barley Ziecheck Medical Offices, in New York, Mojo•Stumer Associates has designed a functional and cost-effective space that extends an immediate welcome to patients. The facility, which includes a reception area, examination rooms, consultation rooms, manager's office and business office, makes the most of its tight budget through crisp, minimal detailing, basic building materials, selective use of wood and marble trim, hospitality-style furnishings, and the doctors' modern art collection to establish a feeling of quality and comfort. Its spatial orientation is straightforward, based on centering the circulation around the spacious waiting room and locating doctors' offices along window walls, simplifying wayfinding for patients and staff alike. Keeping the waiting room airy and open has also yielded an important bonus for the practice. Because the elevator opens directly into the waiting area, the sight of what could easily be perceived as a residential living room comes across as warm and sociable—a sight that patients everywhere wouldn't mind seeing.

Mojo·Stumer Associates

Cline Davis Mann
New York, New York

Even without knowing about Clive Davis Mann, consumers of healthcare products reaffirm its unique position daily as a leading creator of world-class healthcare brands. The New York-based company was founded over 20 years ago as a medical advertising agency, and has developed a specialized organization to guide healthcare brands from prelaunch marketing seeding to end-of-product life cycles. Its command of the field—handling more billion-dollar brands than any other agency serving the healthcare industry—is expressed in two new conference rooms, designed by Mojo•Stumer Associates. Each room, seating 16 or more, is a complex assemblage of IT, A/V, communications and lighting technologies for multi-media presentations. However, what invariably impresses clients is the interior architecture surrounding the high-tech equipment. Fully intended as "knockout" environments, these superbly crafted examples of contemporary cabinetmaking and millwork use the ceiling plane—sarticulated as convex curving soffits and walls—as sculptural motifs. Of course, along with such sleek finishes as wood, leather, stainless steel, aluminum, stone and carpet, there are custom details such as the painted glass panels that double as writing surfaces and pin up boards with clips for pads, demonstrating that form can shape function as well as follow it.

Montroy Andersen DeMarco

Montroy Andersen DeMarco

Givaudan
Corporate Campus
East Hanover, New Jersey

Above: Office/laboratory connection

Upper right: Interior stair

Right: Private offices and teaming area

Below left: Display shelving

Below right: Conference rooms

Opposite: Main atrium

Photography: Paul Warchol

Part office and part laboratory, the sleek new, three-story, 150,000-square-foot facility developed for Givaudan in East Hanover, New Jersey, is paradoxically unified and differentiated in form and function. Founded in 1796 and regarded today as a leader in fragrances and flavors, Vernier, Switzerland-based Givaudan's four-acre corporate campus provides a reception area, corporate offices, marketing showroom, boardroom, training rooms, fragrance libraries, multiple conference rooms for different departments, laboratories, odor booths, three atriums, cafeteria, storage, and telecommunications. What elevates the space, designed by Montroy Andersen DeMarco, above standard corporate interiors are the technical and environmental requirements of the laboratory building, separated from the office building by a centrally located main entrance/reception atrium. For example, by customizing a prefabricated glass system, the design team created odor booths with the requested durability, hermetic seal, environmental conditions and elegant appearance. Givaudan sees a sophisticated aesthetic merging art and science as essential to its industry image. Thus, even the testing center's mechanical components appear as design objects alongside classic modern furnishings and timeless materials such as wood flooring, carpet, stone walkways, glass, metal and concrete to give this world-class company a world-class workplace.

Montroy Andersen DeMarco

U.S. Power Generating Company
New York, New York

Visitors immediately sense a feeling of strength, fluidity and dynamism within the new, one-floor, 10,000-square-foot Manhattan office of U.S. Power Generating Company or USPowerGen, designed by Montroy Andersen DeMarco. That's what USPowerGen is about, after all. Successor to an entity launched in 2003, the company owns and operates 58 generating units at six facilities with a total capacity of over 5,000 megawatts concentrated in metropolitan New York and Boston. In its new facility, comprising reception, conference center, private and open offices, pantry, lounge, IT room and technical support, it requested a design to reflect its identity, create a high comfort level, and support its 45 employees in their varying tasks, responsibilities and privacy needs. The design team responded with glass walls and sliding doors that enclose individual offices and conference rooms without compromising openness and transparency, along with massive sculpted floor-to-ceiling walls finished in distressed, earth-toned steel plate that dramatize such critical locations as the entry, reception area and conference rooms. Finished in

cool, light colors accented by rich earth tones, appointed in functional yet elegantly understated furnishings, and illuminated by a sophisticated lighting design, the contemporary space convincingly portrays USPowerGen flexing its muscles in the energy industry.

Above left: Steel wall

Above: Private office

Left: Reception area with view of open offices

Right: Entry

Opposite top: Conference rooms

Photography: Paul Warchol

Montroy Andersen DeMarco

Montroy Andersen DeMarco
New York, New York

Right: Conference room
Below: Partners' office
Below right: Reception desk
Opposite: Entry, reception and waiting area
Photography: Paul Warchol

Starting in 1990 as a New York-based interior design firm, Montroy Andersen DeMarco has thrived by offering cutting edge space based on the client's vision while remaining within an established budget and consistently devoting a principal to each commission. Promoting innovation and practicality has served the firm well, as shown by the growing numbers of legacy clients, who praise its services and return with new commissions. The design of the new, one-floor, 7,500-square-foot office it has designed for its own 30 employees maximizes the existing space's assets, including high ceilings, tall windows, and south and west exposures, to establish an optimum workplace at a reasonable cost. Accordingly, workstations in the studio have low partitions and shelving and partners' offices and conference rooms are enclosed by clear glass to promote openness, daylight and views, translucent glass separates the reception area from working space to maintain privacy without erecting a visual barrier, noise is controlled at the reception desk with a dropped acoustical ceiling, and a basic white color scheme that is complemented by gray carpet, oak wood flooring, exposed ductwork and exposed concrete helps unify everything, including the library, kitchen and IT area. Who says the shoemaker's children don't wear good shoes?

Montroy ▪ Andersen ▪ DeMarco

Montroy Andersen DeMarco

Christopher Fischer Cashmere
New York, New York

Renowned for producing fine cashmere knitwear with contemporary styling for its own retail stores and for leading stores and labels worldwide, Christopher Fischer Cashmere has opened a new, one-floor, 12,000-square-foot corporate office and showroom in New York where its clothing visually completes the interior design. The space, which has corproate offices as well as a lounge area, kitchen/pantry, private bathrooms and showroom, has been designed by Montroy Andersen DeMarco to provide a cool, minimalist, industrial-chic backdrop for the company's brilliantly

colored offerings when it is not serving as an administrative center. Creating separate zones for work space and showroom that look continuous yet remain discreetly separate to keep interfering functions apart, the design draws on such industrial materials as raw concrete and distressed steel posts, dramatically juxtaposed with elegant light fixtures, modern furniture, lacquered cabinetry and millwork, and interior glass partitions, to act as the perfect foil for stylish attire that wins acclaim from the fashion and business press as well as the patronage of celebrities and socialites.

When Christopher Fischer, an Englishman living in New York, and his colleagues invite the fashion world to do business, here is where the show goes on.

Left: Work area and showroom

Upper left: Freestanding partition in showroom

Below: Showroom facing custom-built library wall that conceals storage and machinery

Photography: Paul Warchol

MSA planning + design

612 Howard Street, Suite 300 • San Francisco, CA 94105 • 415.541.0977 • 415.541.0979 (F)

Two Union Square • 601 Union Street, Suite 4200 • Seattle, WA 98101 • 206.652.3590 • 206.260.3900 (F)

www.msasf.com

MSA planning + design

Bella Pictures
San Francisco, California

Founded by professionals with backgrounds in photo-journalism and e-commerce, Bella Pictures is an innovative company that is transforming the wedding photography industry. The San Francisco headquarters recently turned to MSA planning + design to design their corporate office to reflect its progressive, team-oriented culture. Bella wanted to showcase the

photography of their award winning photojournalists while simultaneously creating an exciting workspace that fosters flexibility while accommodating new trends and styles. The resulting one-floor, 15,000-square-foot facility in San Francisco's Financial District's historic Adam Grant Building (1908) provides an environment that is dramatic, open, and clean

while successfully meeting Bella's budget and schedule. The project was completed in just three months for only $73 per square foot. Among the reasons for its success is the incorporation of existing historic building components, mid-century classic modern design with 21st century workplace needs. The company's photography is displayed in gallery-like installations

to showcase its services. Bella welcomes clients in comfortable, casual, comfort. The living room-styled client lounge features the mix of mid-century classic modern furnishings and contemporary pieces used throughout the facility. The space includes private offices, workstations, breakout meeting areas, conference rooms, a videography studio, and lunch rooms in a

team-oriented office environment where 110 employees with different needs and job functions can enjoy both privacy and openness. Gene Domecus, CFO, Bella Pictures, declares, "It's perfect," ". . . they exceeded my expectations."

Top right: Private office
Top far right: Conference room
Right: Marketing
Far right: Breakout area
Below left: Hall
Below right: Elevator lobby
Bottom left: Client lounge
Bottom right: Entrance
Photography: Mark Compton

131

MSA planning + design

Macy's, Inc.
Macys.com
San Francisco, California

Below: Executive reception

Bottom left: 9th Floor break room

Bottom right: Workstation broad band divider

Right: Break out area

Opposite lower right: 8th floor elevator lobby

Opposite bottom right: 8th floor Lobby

Photography: Mark Compton

While Macy's, the nation's largest department store chain, was founded in 1858, its online business, Macys.com, dates back only to 1997. Thus, when Macys.com sought a new home for 294 employees in San Francisco, it asked MSA planning + design to design a dramatic, open and modern environment that could compete with other Bay Area companies for talent, departing from Macy's traditional retail image but still reflecting its brand. The project was complicated by the darkness, low ceilings and interior columns in the historic Monadnock Building (1906) where Macys.com located. In updating the building, MSA transformed it into an open, light filled environment. Renovation included removing barriers and exposing ceilings to raise elevations. Brightly colored open "broadband" portals are used throughout, dividing work areas, allowing light, air and communication to flow uninterrupted. Color is used as an identifying element for each floor (red, blue, green) and to break up furniture layouts. In response to the IT Professionals' needs for informality in the workplace, MSA created multiple break-out meeting areas where social interaction is unavoidable and new ideas flow freely and where the staff can get away from their desks, eat, socialize and relax. Kent Anderson, CEO, Macys.com, reports, "Our team thrives in our new space. The design has had a tremendous positive effect, facilitating high energy, high levels of interaction and collaboration between all members of our team"

MSA planning + design

Macy's, Inc.
Macy's Furniture Gallery Washington Square
Portland, Oregon

Home furnishings retailing has come a long way from the dreary rows of sofas found in traditional furniture stores. At Macy's Furniture Gallery Washington Square, in Portland, Oregon, MSA planning + design has demonstrated how effectively today's contextual approach works by turning a former electronics store into an inviting, two-story, 15,120-square-foot residential-style environment. A few critical modifications equipped the existing structure for its new mission, including installing a new residential-style entrance, reconfiguring vertical circulation by installing a new central escalator well, three exit stairs, passenger elevator, freight elevator, and expanding the existing dock. The unsound skylight above the escalator well was replaced with a double recessed coved lighting element that

draws the eye and customers up to the second floor. To provide an elegant and adaptable environment for residential furnishings of varying forms and styles, the selling floors feature carpeted open spaces divided by colorful freestanding focal walls that frame home-like vignettes. There are wide circulation paths paved in white porcelain tile, and an easily recognizable customer service desk where customers and sales representatives can sit comfortably and semi-privately. Customers are treated like houseguests at Macy's Furniture Gallery Washington Square, exploring rooms they can actually take home. Tom Polich, VP Capital Projects and Store Planning says, "MSA is a pleasure to do business with. I recommend their services, and would welcome the opportunity to work with them in the future."

Left: Customer service desk

Lower left: Escalator well

Below: View along circulation path

Opposite upper left: Typical vignette

Opposite upper right: Entrance

Photography: Mark Compton

MSA planning + design

University of California, San Francisco Medical Center
Outpatient Pediatric Rehabilitation and Blood Center
San Francisco, California

Called one of America's top 10 hospitals by *U.S. News & World Report*, University of California, San Francisco Medical Center is known for compassionate and innovative care. Keeping its facilities as modern as its services, the Center recently opened the Outpatient Pediatric Rehabilitation and the Blood Center,

both designed by MSA planning + design. While the two spaces shared the same tight schedule, each had different requirements. In the Pediatric facility, the design had to accommodate injured and stressed children, and add a therapeutic pool without making strutural changes. For the Blood Center, the needs

included storage for medical supplies and collected blood, and privacy for blood donors in an open area. MSA's designs reflect an attention to detail, creative problem solving, and client involvement. The Pediatric pool was placed over an existing beam on the floor below. A Pediatric "play house"

reception area was created to comfort children. In the Blood Center, a partition/ room divider was devised to separate technicians from the waiting area, and glass blocks were installed in the Blood Center's reception wall to compensate for San Francisco's famed gray days with borrowed light to diffuse the

view of an adjacent fast food restaurant—thus implementing good design.

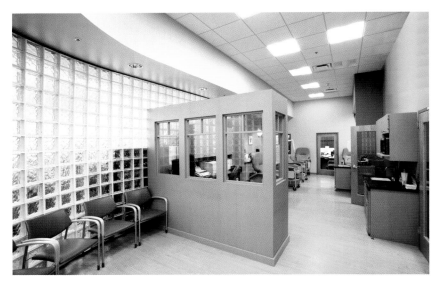

Above: Blood Center reception

Above right: Pediatric reception

Below: Signage

Right: Pediatric therapeutic pool

Photography: Mark Compton

NELSON

The Lacek Group
Minneapolis, Minnesota

While advertising agencies frequently maintain entertaining areas for clients, The Lacek Group's new client accommodations included an unusual prerequisite. The agency asked NELSON to design them as part of a four-floor, 42,000-square-foot renovation and expansion in which the company's 120 employees would work uninterrupted in their Minneapolis office. To plan construction, the project was broken into four phases and strict deadlines and schedule milestones were established to suit employees and clients. Not surprisingly, the remodeled, contemporary-style facility, which includes the reception area, conference rooms, private offices, open workstations, pantry and restrooms, is highlighted by the "Skybox" client entertaining area and integrating staircase, reflecting a new focus on public and client-facing areas. Since the 19th floor has direct access to an outdoor deck, it was the obvious location for the "Skybox," which incorporates a catering kitchen with stone counters and metal laminate cabinetry, lounge area showcasing a glass-and-cherry custom fireplace and skyline views, and dining areas with leather-and-mohair banquette seating. But the remainder of the facility also shines, thanks to spacious open areas, vivid colors, comfortable modern furnishings, and the company's glass art collection. As a Lacek Group representative notes, "We are delighted with the results, which truly show for themselves."

Top right: Reception desk
Left: Skybox fireplace lounge
Above: Skybox dining area
Opposite: Reception area
Photography: Paul Crosby

NELSON

Strother Communications
Minneapolis, Minnesota

Ornate woodwork, coffered ceilings and a sense of history were all abandoned when Strother Communications, a public relations firm, vacated the venerable Foshay Tower, in downtown Minneapolis, to occupy the 41st floor penthouse of the Campbell Mithun Building.

But the new, one-floor, 4,894-square-foot modern office, designed by NELSON for 25 employees, has its own triumphant story to tell. The drama begins when visitors ride one of eight elevators to the 40th floor sky lobby and take a small private elevator to the penthouse. Here the design

galvanizes its long, narrow space by exploiting the surrounding vistas with glass walls or clerestory windows, creating a sense of unlimited transparency. The view isn't everything, of course. The front corridor's wood millwork displays Patrick and Patricia Strother's world-class art collection. A consistently

high level of design lets the entire office function as both public space and work space, so one area flows gracefully into another, accompanied by sophisticated lighting. There's even a client telephone booth sporting a Superman logo on its sliding glass door and a glowing acid green "kryptonite" wall panel

above the purple aggregate glass countertop, urging people to have fun as the Man of Steel surely would so high above Minneapolis.

Above left: Art installation beneath company mantra, "Change Minds"

Above right: Conference room

Left: Private office and open work area

Opposite: Creative meeting room

Photography: Dana Wheelock

NELSON

Educational Credit Management Corporation
(ECMC)
St. Paul, Minnesota

Four hundred employees of Educational Credit Management Corporation assigned to the company's St. Paul campus may be among the fortunate white collar workers in America who can truthfully say their office is good for their health. In fact, two floors in ECMC's Main Building and one floor in a second building,

encompassing 110,000 square feet, have been purposefully renovated to demonstrate that a healthier workforce will have less absenteeism, lower health insurance costs and higher productivity. Starting with a stringent budget, ECMC, a non-profit national guaranty agency that insures student loans under the Federal

Family Education Loan Program, retained NELSON to design a work environment that promotes the health of its staff while supporting the agency's strategic, organizational, functional, cultural and financial platforms. The resulting floors, which include reception, conference center (boardroom and adjacent conference areas),

executive offices, executive pantry, coffee areas, workrooms, ancillary conference rooms, teaming areas, open office, computer rooms, restrooms, full-service health facility (martial arts studio, aerobics studio, fitness center, shower and locker rooms), full-service cafeteria with kitchen, and training rooms, represent a major

culture shift for ECMC. Key to the renovation has been the holistic approach to supporting employee health in the workplace that NELSON developed with the company. Identifying all employee touch points, the design team treated the workplace, public spaces and state-of-the-art gym facility as a continuous environment where being

Top: Coffee area
Left: Boardroom
Above: Teaming area
Photography: Paul Crosby

active, losing weight, and improving psychological and physical health are legitimate on-the-job activities along with work assignments. To advance this idea, the facility encourages the staff to move around during the day by providing specialized settings designed to support a wide range of office tasks. Besides introducing personal walking workstations, representing an alternative workspace model to the standard workstation, the space offers such options as conference spaces, small group gathering areas, kitchens and break rooms to help employees work more effectively. Close consultation with ECMC, aided by constant monitoring of quality, cost and scheduling, ensured that the project met its projected goals. Consequently, ECMC has a colorful, cost-effective and inviting modern environment that truly resonates with its new corporate culture—and its workforce.

Right: Fitness center
Below: Small group gathering area

OWP/P | Cannon Design

111 West Washington Street, Suite 2100 • Chicago, IL 60602 • 312.332.9600 • 312.332.9601 (F)

www.cannondesign.com

OWP/P | Cannon Design

The Marketing Store
Lombard, Illinois

Located in Lombard, Illinois, a Chicago suburb close to McDonald's headquarters, The Marketing Store creates toys, games and packaging for McDonald's Happy Meals as well as products for Coca Cola, General Mills and other leading corporations. Problem was, its two major operations, advertising and product development, were divided into separate office locations and cultures. A recent, one-floor, 80,000-square-foot renovation, designed by OWP/P | Cannon Design, not only united 190 employees,

it helped jumpstart their creative output. The sleek, contemporary space might never have materialized, since the lease had three years remaining. However, an early exit made no financial sense. So OWP/P | Cannon Design's makeover was temporary, economical and effective. To give the advertising group a polished downtown agency look, and to support the product development group with a creative and collaborative workspace, the renovation opened up the floor, placing new, informal collaborative areas furnished

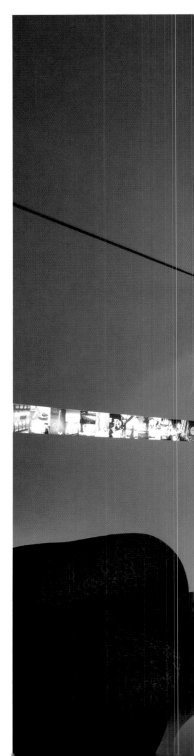

with existing soft seating on main circulation paths, creating a stylish reception area, and turning the little-used cafeteria into an oasis for creative meetings. Despite numerous project constraints, the employees insist the new space has raised their energy, morale and output.

Better yet, their newest work is winning plaudits from McDonald's and awards from peers.

Left: Collaboration space

Below: Reception

Opposite center: Entry

Opposite bottom left: Collaboration space

Photography: Christopher Barrett/Hedrich Blessing

OWP/P | Cannon Design

Cannon Design
The Power House
St. Louis, Missouri

The Power House, originally developed to provide coal-fired steam heat to buildings in downtown St. Louis, is the kind of historic structure that many admire but few can use. Fortunately, after being decommissioned and vacated in 1980, the Power House was purchased by Cannon Design in 2005 and transformed into the firm's regional headquarters. Overseeing the design, development and construction of the restoration, renovation and adaptive reuse of the voluminous structure, Cannon Design created an award-winning environment for its employees that is intuitive, collaborative and open. The design features a three-story gallery formed by constructing two partial levels to combine with two existing levels and provide 32,000 square feet of office and conference space. Besides facilitating Cannon Design's team-oriented approach to practice, the new space is unapologetically spectacular. Floors are set back from the expansive windows and monumental walls to maintain a sense of transparency and volume, and every major interior component, encompassing HVAC, plumbing and electrical infrastructure, meets current life safety and LEED standards, resulting in LEED Gold certification. Award citations note that the Power House portrays the best of both worlds, the historic one that created it long ago, and the modern one that sustains it today.

Above left: Interior structure

Above right: Exterior

Far left: Conference room with restored window

Left: Three-story gallery

Opposite: View of gallery and set back

Photography: Gayle Babcock

Decades of executive leadership and staff operations on a singular campus have yielded to a new, 11-story, 250,000-square-foot world headquarters in downtown Chicago for a Fortune 500 Company. This major relocation, implemented to empower managers to make day-to-day decisions and free the executive team to focus on big-picture, strategic long-range planning, has been closely supported by the new interior build-out, designed by OWP/P | Cannon Design. Consequently, the extensive accommodations, which include the executive offices and support spaces, boardroom, multi-use conferencing facility, executive dining space and break areas, along with private offices, open workstations, conference rooms, coffee bars, casual encounter spaces, and large café/auditorium, represent a deliberate departure from the company's historic use of physical space

Right: Corridor with view into coffee/copy area

Below: Reception

Opposite upper left: Executive dining

Opposite upper right: Interior stair

Opposite bottom left: Elevator lobby

Photography: Christopher Barrett/Hedrich Blessing

OWP/P | Cannon Design

and projection of corporate identity. By selectively combining privacy and openness through such spaces as private offices with gradient frosted glass fronts, open workstations, and a wide range of private and public areas for formal and informal meetings, the new office environment gives executives their required privacy while increasing transparency in the workplace to encourage interaction. Equally important, it has enabled the company to establish itself in a new location as a world-class organization and industry leader, able to attract the very best talent and to host business leaders in an appropriate setting. A simple, powerful and refined space designed to evoke the values of light, shadow and sky, the new headquarters uses such sleek materials as polished stone, clear, back-painted, and frosted glass, carpet, metal and classic modern furnishings, all keyed to a color palette of whites and light grays, to capture the sense of being within clouds.

Far left: Conference room
Below left: Reception desk
Below: Stair detail

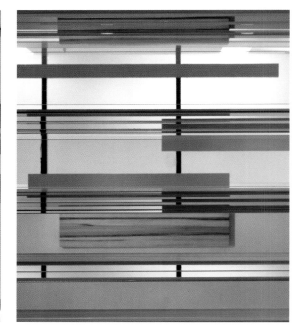

Perkins+Will

Perkins+Will

Cardinal Health
Dublin, Ohio

Growing demand for its products has prompted Cardinal Health, a major global manufacturer and distributor of medical and surgical supplies, to examine its own well-being by expanding its headquarters in Dublin, Ohio. To leverage Cardinal's systems, talent, and cross-functional teaming, and to sustain continuity and connection during changes resulting from ongoing reorganization and acquisitions, the design team engaged the institution's executives and general staff in a series of dialogues to examine how design could better support key business processes. Cardinal's new 4-floor, 250,000-square-foot facility for 1,000 employees is the result of this intense interaction. The facility takes Cardinal in a new direction by extending beyond the existing East Campus via a pedestrian bridge across a wooded ravine. In addition, such facilities as the lobby, open office areas, private offices, meeting spaces, fitness center, cafeteria, and credit union give staff members a variety of work experiences and supportive environments to serve evolving needs, creating a bright, airy, and inviting atmosphere with attractive, contemporary furnishings, exceptional wayfinding, and stellar outdoor views that should keep Cardinal's headquarters operations in excellent health for a long time.

Clockwise from upper left: Lobby, private offices and workstations, coffee bar, office corridor, cafeteria

Opposite top: Conference room

Photography: Brad Feinkopf, Feinkopf Photography

Perkins+Will　　Haworth, Inc.
One Haworth Center
Holland, Michigan

When Haworth, a global manufacturer of adaptable workspaces, decided to emphasize design in repositioning its brand, Perkins+Will spearheaded an integrated, multidisciplinary approach that addressed the firm's core business objectives: implementing sustainability, growing market share, enhancing the customer experience, and maintaining a progressive workplace. The transformation entailed stripping the 250,000-square-foot building to its structural frame, then rebuilding it with a 50,000-square-foot addition. The resulting three-floor, contemporary facility truly demonstrates how

design advances business goals. Designed to reflect Haworth's values, culture, and brand platform, the new space features Adaptable Workspaces, which allow the world-class facility to function as a product demonstration "lab." This "chassis" is organized into "dynamic" (open office), "temporal" (rooms of movable partitions), and "place" (permanent infrastructure) zones. Another key feature—a striking, 45,000-square-foot, L-shaped atrium flooded with natural light—was devised to boost employee morale, positively affect customers, and incorporate sustainability practices. Balconies

extending into the space boast employee interaction areas and customer experience zones, and the atrium's plant-covered roof reduces heat gain. Additional use of renewable resources and considerable efforts to divert waste from landfills helped the building earn a LEED Gold certification. This award-winning project effectively harmonized integrated brand, workspace strategies and sustainable design. The resulting environment both eloquently narrates Haworth's story and meets the company's broader business goals.

Clockwise from top left:
Entrance and atrium, exterior, global resource library, welcome center, view across bridge

Opposite: Atrium

Photography: Steven Hall and Craig Dugan/Hedrich Blessing, Curt Clayton/Clayton Studios

Perkins+Will

The PrivateBank and Trust Company Headquarters
Chicago, Illinois

Founded in 1989, the PrivateBank and Trust Company wants to be the bank of choice for middle-market commercial and commercial real estate companies, as well as business owners, executives, entrepreneurs, and families in the markets and communities it serves in 34 cities across 10 states. To win market acceptance of its comprehensive suite of personal and commercial banking, treasury management, investment products, capital markets, private banking, and wealth management services, the institution focuses on building strong relationships with clients. Its new, two-floor, 76,000-square-foot contemporary headquarters, located in the heart of Chicago's financial district, is designed accordingly. The facility's strong architectural foundation, drawing inspiration from the context of the building, is anchored by a dramatic central banking hall and a monumental open stairway, which are complemented in turn by an elegant and welcoming interior of natural materials, warm colors, comfortable furnishings, and subtle lighting. Everything clients see, from the reception area to the sit-down tellers' stations, banking platform, executive offices, conference center, and client lounge—a parlor where client meetings can be held—attests to the PrivateBank's power and flexibility in delivering top quality financial services with a personal touch.

Above left: Conference room
Above: Reception
Far left: Executive offices
Left: Corridor
Opposite: Banking hall
Photography: Craig Dugan/ Hedrich Blessing

Perkins+Will

Perkins+Will Miami Office
Miami, Florida

An architect's office is often a laboratory for new ideas and a showroom for clients as well as a workplace for architects. That's why Perkins+Will has turned its new, one-floor, 7,700-square-foot office for 50 employees in Coral Gables, Florida, into a state-of-the-art, sustainable and cost-effective workplace. The largely open environment, which includes reception, conference/war rooms, open studio, materials/reference library and employee lounge, focuses on giving occupants a flexible and reconfigurable space that is also sustainable. To meet these goals, Perkins+Will has developed a floor plan that minimizes permanent walls, uses glass for partitions, including demountable

ones for the conference/war rooms, employs workstations with partitions that are low and easily adaptable, and provides shelving on casters so the materials/reference library can be shifted as needed. To achieve sustainability in an uncertified existing building, the design team has worked with the building manager and maintenance crew on building operations

and taken such measures as exposing concrete floors and ceilings, reusing existing built-in bookcases, maximizing daylight, and installing Green Guard-certified furnishings. The rewards for this effort include a 45 percent reduction in power consumption, LEED CI Gold certification and a classic modern interior that impresses both employees and visitors.

Above left in descending order: Boardroom, studio view of conference rooms

Above: Open studio

Left: Reception showcasing branded wall

Photography: Mark Surloff

Powers Brown Architecture

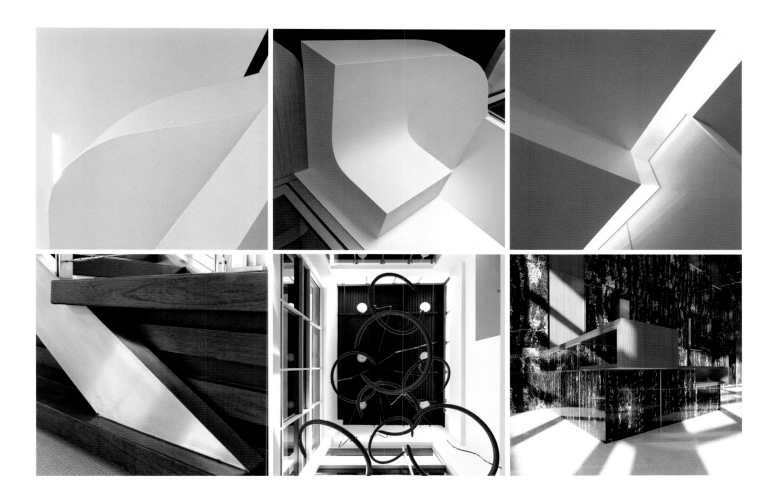

1314 Texas Ave., 2nd Floor • Houston, TX 77002 • 713.224.0456 • 713.224.0457 (F)

www.powersbrown.com

Powers Brown Architecture

Logica
Houston, Texas

Design can transform an organization in numerous, far-reaching ways, as the North American head-quarters of London-based Logica, located in Houston, memorably demonstrates. Designed by Powers Brown Architecture, the new, one-floor, 18,000-square-foot office gives this leading IT and business services company an up-to-date workplace for its evolving high-tech operations and state-of-the-art persona. Responsible for site selection as well as programming and interior architecture, Powers Brown has produced a facility comprising private offices, open office area, conference rooms, demonstration rooms,

break rooms, and lounge where 64 employees can openly interact and clients clearly enjoy the modern environment. The project began when Powers Brown produced multiple test fit solutions based on the potential of available build-ings to meet Logica's needs. Once Logica chose a building with an L-shaped floorplate, the design team created a sleek, contemporary space with views in three direc-tions to supply the daylight required by the company. One signature element, the innovative, three-dimensional wall design that integrates storage, work surfaces and writing surfaces, keeps the space as open as possible

at the same time it projects a sophisticated, futuristic image, coolly portrayed in white and gray with "Logica yellow" accents, that's as distinctive as Logica itself.

Above right: Lounge

Right: Reception desk

Below left: Conference room

Below right: Open office area with hoteling wall

Opposite: View of break room from open office area

Photography: Dror Baldinger

Powers Brown Architecture

Seismic Exchange, Inc.
Houston, Texas

Seismic Exchange, Inc. knew that relocating its headquarters from New Orleans, where it was founded in 1975, to Houston after Hurricane Katrina, would be emotional and complicated. That's why the seismic data marketing firm, which serves the oil and gas industry, requested the feel of the social scene in New Orleans in its new, freestanding, five-floor, 73,000-square-foot home office for 200 employees, designed by Powers Brown Architecture. Compelled by the idea, Powers Brown developed a visual language for the urban ecology Seismic Exchange that could be expressed in its new modern structure without mimicking the French Quarter. The resulting private offices, open office areas, conference rooms, lounge and café break rooms balance respect for individual privacy with receptivity to formal and chance encounters by creating both lively public meeting spots and quiet private areas where public space discreetly intrudes. A dynamic design accented by double-height spaces on several floors and exposed post-tensioned floorplates, it also draws on such timeless materials as limestone, travertine, wood, metal and glass, along with attention-getting light bands and recessed circular light fixtures, to help Seismic Exchange feel at home again. Company spokesperson Rivie Cary declares, "The building exceeds our early expectations."

Far left: Conference room

Left: Upper level monument stair

Lower far left: Café

Lower left: Lavatory

Above: Third floor reception

Opposite bottom: Lobby and corridor

Photography: Dror Baldinger

Powers Brown Architecture

Office Pavilion
Houston, Texas

The Site for Office Pavillion's Distribution HQ in Houston was chosen primarily for its visibility from two highly traveled highway corridors. Located at the intersection of Beltway 8 North and Highway 290 with multiple overpasses offering elevated views down to the building, the design had to incorporate visual interest from the roof down. We used a horizontal massing strategy for the exterior of the building with functional sunshading devices and an articulated roof with clerestory areas to light the interior. These dominant horizontal elements from the exterior resonate to the building's interior as exhibition walls for Office Pavillion's products in the lobby. The interior is designed as if all of its furnishings, although functional for administrative employees, are on display. We used full height frameless glass partitions throughout the interior to showcase Office Pavillion's various products behind.

Below left: Glass box conference room
Above right: Mezzanine conference room
Right: Lobby waiting area
Below right: Showroom
Opposite: Lobby
Photography: Dror Baldinger

Powers Brown Architecture

The Plaza at Enclave Parkway
Houston, TX

How did the shell and core of a new, six-story, 354,000-square-foot office building developed as a major corporate headquarters by Core Real Estate LLC, occupying an infill site in a now-full master development in Houston, rise above the banality that typifies suburban commercial investment buildings? Instead of the 12-story building that would have been constructed on the development's awkwardly sized last parcel in a conventional market scenario, the imaginative Plaza at Enclave Parkway, designed by Powers Brown Architecture, uses an expansive, Z-shaped floorplate that establishes two internal zones. One hides the functional loading area, while the other accommodates a serene courtyard garden. The garden, paved in travertine and animated by water flowing from limestone fountains, continuously defines the experience of tenants and visitors, from the moment they leave the parking garage to pass through the stately loggia and enter the soaring lobby, where the monumental Porturo marble wall reprises the garden theme. Another benefit of the Z-shaped floorplate is its thoughtful configuration. Minimal depth, careful site placement and solar orientation—part of the sustainable design strategy behind the project's LEED Gold certification—bring natural light and outdoor views deep inside the office pods, amenities office workers everywhere can appreciate.

Top right: Elevator lobby

Above left: Outdoor café seating

Above right: Corridor with garden view

Left: Lobby with Porturo marble wall

Photography: Dror Baldinger

Rottet Studio

808 Travis, Suite 100 • Houston, TX 77002 • 713.221.1830 • 713.221.1858 (F)

555 S. Flower, Suite 700 • Los Angeles, CA 90071 • 213.612.4585 • 213.612.4373 (F)

180 Varick, Suite 440 • New York, NY 10014 • 212.537.9245

98 Battery, Suite 500 • San Francisco, CA 94111 • 415.398.3916

20645 North Pima, Suite 220 • Scottsdale, AZ 85288 • 480.419.8877

www.rottetstudio.com • 866.629.4284

Rottet Studio

Artis Capital Management
San Francisco, California

Far left: Private office

Left: Interior corridor with art

Below: Conference room with stone and carpet detail

Opposite upper left and right: Trading desk, gym

Opposite bottom: Entrance

Photography: Eric Laignel

Acknowledging the intense and visually stimulating nature of its work, Artis Capital Management retained Lauren Rottet—in a Project of Lauren Rottet while with DMJM Rottet—to design a one floor, 16,625-square-foot office in San Francisco as a home-like, contemporary environment for its 15 employees. The stunning new facility, comprising private offices, conference rooms, reception area, art galleries, entertainment bar and gym, embraces the investment management company's belief that contemporary art is "extremely important" to its culture by making art the focal point. Yet the design is clearly a workplace. Each employee's workstation is customized to balance comfort and productivity, a gym equipped with private showers, massage room and lounge chairs provides relaxation, and art is installed unobtrusively in the "white box," a visually quiet atmosphere that counteracts the intensity of computer screens with such details as the perimeter wall, untouched by interior walls to promote clear views of San Francisco Bay, the dark gray cleft stone encircling custom carpet, evoking water lapping a shore, and incisions in the ceilings, exposing wood reveals, and soft, ambient lighting. A company representative notes, "While the space is beautiful for the visitor to observe, it is most importantly a well-planned, inspiring environment for our employees."

Rottet Studio

Mattel Design Center
El Segundo, California

Every business knows what can happen to even the finest premises over time, as Mattel Design Center, the toy design studio of Mattel, Inc., the world's largest toy company, can attest. Having inhabited its building in El Segundo, California for 20-plus years, the Design Center found the space closed in, disorganized and at odds with major changes in technology, building codes and its own design process. Lauren Rottet—in a Project of Lauren Rottet while with DMJM Rottet—designed a total renovation for the Design Center, working against a limited budget and uninterruptible operations

to give the two-floor, 199,975-square-foot facility new private offices, workstations, reception, presentation theater, model shop, chemical laboratory, fabric printing, Boxology laboratory, mail and reprographics center, cafeteria and outdoor dining. Not only does the renovation resolve such challenges as maximizing collaborative work areas while accommodating the extensive storage needed for toy design, allowing offices, cafeteria and toy manufacturing plant to coexist safely by establishing three air handling zones, developing custom-designed workstations with a noted furniture manufacturer to

satisfy Mattel designers, and clarifying circulation using a flexible floor plan of "streets," "neighborhoods" and conveniently located services, the new environment is

functional, user-friendly and attractive—vital matters to occupants who are designers themselves.

Left: New dining area

Below left: Ramp to presentation theater and display wall with chronology of Mattel catalog covers in Town Square

Below : "Town Square" reception desk

Right: Cafeteria seating along light wall

Photography: Victor Muschetto

"The future belongs to those who believe in the beauty of their dreams."
Eleanor Roosevelt

"Don't be afraid to give up the good to go for the great."
John D. Rockefeller

"Imagination is intelligence having fun."
Anonymous

MATTEL

Rottet Studio

MidFirst Bank
3030 Camelback
Phoenix, Arizona

MidFirst Bank, a privately owned, Oklahoma-based bank founded in 1982 that has become one of the nation's 100 largest banks, recently asked Rottet Studio—in a Project of Lauren Rottet while with DMJM Rottet—to design a branded environment in Phoenix to help it stand out from rivals in entering the competitive Arizona market. As a result, customers have paid attention since opening day to MidFirst's 4,000-square-foot full-service branch bank at 3030 Camelback, part of its two-floor, 27,000-square-foot office at this location. The dramatic and inviting facility stretches a branch bank's budget to evoke traditional Southwestern interiors with expansive, open areas, meticulous details, such distinctive materials as olive wood veneer, stone and hemp wallcoverings, and residential-style furnishings, relying on local vendors and hand-selected materials to control costs. MidFirst has exploited its premises thoroughly, dedicating one-quarter of the first floor to the branch bank, arranging the remaining space, including private perimeter offices, interior workstations, conference rooms, break rooms, security vault, mailroom and restrooms, around a two-story

Left: Lobby with stone fireplace, lounge and teller stations

Above: Small reception area

Opposite top: Vault

Photography: Eric Laignel

175

Rottet Studio

corporate lobby and new interconnecting stair and elevator, and installing overhangs on the south and west facades along with automatic shades to capture daylight with minimal heat gain. To give the branch bank visibility from passing vehicular traffic, the design even inserts a new façade onto the existing building. MidFirst's appreciation for the design ("Bravo, customers like it!") is reflected in Rottet Studio's repeat work for the bank at several other locations.

Above left: Corridor with private offices

Above: Staircase to second level

Left: Custom reception desk

Space Design Incorporated

Space Design Incorporated

Nonprofit Foundation
New York, New York

Right: View of main conference room from reception

Below: Reception waiting area

Bottom: Elevator lobby

Opposite: Interconnecting stair, reception and open area

Photography: Tom Crane Photography, Inc.

A new, two-floor, 15,000-square-foot contemporary office near the top of a premier property on Manhattan's legendary Fifth Avenue offering panoramic views of Midtown, Central Park and the Plaza Hotel is even more rewarding for the 43 employees of a Nonprofit Foundation because they all share its views and daylight. To satisfy the Foundation's request that the skyline should be visible from every workspace, Space Design Incorporated has designed a traditional floor plan—comprising reception area, private offices, administrative support workstations, board room, informal conference areas, interconnecting stair, data/server room, coffee area and copy/mail area—with a twist. Private offices have glass fronts and workstations have low panels to admit daylight and spectacular views deep inside the space. The interiors are refreshingly contemporary as well, balancing forward-looking forms with timeless, dignified materials. As a result, a material palette of classic camel, black granite and rich walnut is combined with black-painted existing dark mahogany and furniture finished in quarter cut walnut veneer, anodized aluminum and brushed stainless steel to give the Foundation a timely new image. "Everyone enjoys the work environment," notes the Foundation's executive vice president. "Space Design was extremely professional, talented and insightful, and made the project a great success."

Space Design Incorporated

Quaker Chemical
Headquarters and Laboratory Facilities
Conshohocken, Pennsylvania

While corporate America abandons many aging industrial buildings, Quaker Chemical responded differently when its 1929 chemical plant, in Conshohocken, Pennsylvania, ceased manufacturing. Quaker, a global provider of process chemicals, chemical specialties, and technical services, moved its headquarters from an on-site 1960s office building to the former plant. In designing the new headquarters, Space Design Incorporated called for complete gutting, exposing and sandblasting brick and wood beams and refurbishing elevator cabs and massive steel sliding doors to revive their historic imagery, in addition to installing new exterior glazing, doors and roofing, MEP systems, and lavatories. The two-floor, 75,000-square-foot headquarters, part of a 100,000-square-foot renovation that restores a four-floor, 24,000-square-foot building for new laboratories, offers 150 employees numerous settings, including reception, collaborative spaces, open workstations, private offices, boardroom, respite spaces, wellness center and cafeteria with outdoor dining. Floor plans follow conventional layouts, but the interiors, contrasting brick and wood with clear-coated and black-painted steel, polished chrome and bold colors, and incorporating slate tile, modular carpet and contemporary furnishings, are anything but conventional. To quote Ron Naples, Quaker's chairman of the board, "Although enclosed by powerful reminders of Quaker's deep heritage in industrial America, the office is a complete 21st-century high-tech workplace."

Above: Second floor sitting area

Top right: Second floor open workstation area

Above right: Manager's workstation

Right: Elevator with original steel doors

Opposite: First floor reception and main stair

Photography: Tom Crane Photography, Inc.

Space Design Incorporated

Space Design Incorporated
Philadelphia, Pennsylvania

Having served greater Philadelphia since 1975, Space Design Incorporated is an architecture and design firm that knows the value clients place on daylight and views. So when the firm designed the latest office for itself, a one-floor, 7,500-square-foot space for 25 employees atop the historic Curtis Center in Center City, it decided that the spectacular views from windows overlooking Washington Square, the Delaware River and Center City should be shared by all through the placement of walkways instead of walls along the windows. The decision energizes the entire facility, including the reception area, 4,200-square-foot open design studio and resource library, private offices, administrative support area, display areas, multi-purpose presentation room, conference rooms, coffee areas, and central plotter/copy/mail area, by bringing sunshine and the skyline deep inside. However, the contemporary interior has a distinct personality of its own. New and existing furnishings, such new materials as black granite tile, carpet tile, textiles and dark expresso-painted woodwork, and elements re-used from the firm's former space, including the reception desk, glass and wood doors, millwork and carpet, come together in a "green" design strategy that has saved costs and given Space Design Incorporated a desirable workplace that is uniquely its own.

Above left: Library looking toward studio

Above: Studio and library

Below left: Reception looking toward studio

Below: Workstations overlooking 12-story atrium

Opposite: Reception desk

Photography: Tom Crane Photography, Inc.

Space Design Incorporated

Morgan Stanley
West Conshohocken, Pennsylvania

Above: Corridor gallery outside conference room

Left: Typical reception area, opening to conference room with sliding doors

Lower left: Typical conference room with translucent panels to corridor gallery outside

Photography: Tom Crane Photography, Inc.

How do you keep 580 employees at Morgan Stanley's eight-floor, 130,000-square-foot facility in West Conshohocken, Pennsylvania, connected with each other and the hub of business activity? The successful design solution for Morgan Stanley, one of the world's largest diversified financial services companies, has been conceived by Space Design Incorporated as a traditional office with perimeter private offices and central support staff areas that revolves around a central interconnecting stair. This circulation artery provides easy access between work groups and proximity to the critical, centrally located trading room. Outfitted for efficiency, each work group's accommodations contain free-floating file alcoves and a free-floating "equipment pod" that discreetly houses and conceals copiers, printers, fax machines and supplies. However, the design transcends basic efficiency by establishing a light, natural and contemporary environment that features ash wood doors, frames and built-in cabinetry, white-lacquered wall panels, sand-colored carpet, sandblasted glass and sophisticated direct and indirect lighting—a perfect, gallery-like backdrop for classic modern furniture and the client's fine art collection. Commenting on his firm's 20-year relationship with Space Design Incorporated, Phillip Heaver, Morgan Stanley vice president, facilities management, declares, "Space Design created an elegant and sophisticated contemporary design which reflects Morgan Stanley's image and forward thinking."

Staffelbach

Staffelbach Kosmos Energy
Dallas, Texas

Visitors realize they are experiencing an extraordinary space the moment they enter the one-floor, 50,663-square-foot office in Dallas designed by Staffelbach for 120 employees of Kosmos Energy, an international oil and gas company. James C. Musselman, an executive of Kosmos, knows exactly why this happens. "Kosmos Energy is an independent oil and gas exploration and production company operating in West Africa," he explains, "so it was important that our new headquarters reflected both our technical creativity and African cultures. The professionals at Staffelbach accomplished this objective beyond our expectations, designing an interior that integrated our West African art and artifacts into a beautiful, functional working

Right: Credenza and wall paneling details in boardroom
Below: Boardroom
Opposite: Drum Room
Photography: Nick Merrick/ Hedrich Blessing

environment. As members of the Kosmos team, they provided incomparable service, ensuring our move-in was flawless and attending to every detail." The contemporary space, featuring private offices, boardroom, conference areas, reception, gallery, workspaces and support areas, achieves its unique ambiance by balancing the company's respect for the African cultures where it does business, hiring and training local residents and minimizing the company's footprint on the environment, with the everyday needs of Dallas employees. Starting with an efficient floor plan defined by axis points that connect to the main lobby, the design draws on earthy, warm and inviting colors inspired by the West African landscape, natural and recycled materials highlighted by African hardwoods, bold and simply detailed architectural forms and sophisticated, energy-efficient lighting to create an atmosphere not unlike the gracious home of a knowledgeable collector of African art. Public areas, for example, are characterized by the gallery, whose museum-

Above: Conference room

Left: Meeting space outside conference room

Staffelbach

like setting invites guests to relax and enjoy its authentic and distinctive pieces of African art. By comparison, private areas are represented by the employees' multi-purpose room, which is inviting, warm and calming on a more intimate scale, like a kitchen everyone gravitates to. Meticulous detailing assures that the company's brand is expressed at every opportunity. The choice of zebrawood from Central Africa's Cameroon and Congo for many walls, for example, enriches the interiors with the heavy, hard wood's pronounced grain,

Above right: Details of furnishings in pre-function area

Right: Gallery

Opposite: Pre-function area before boardroom

Staffelbach

while the addition of sapele, a wood native to tropical Africa, exploits its darker grain to make doorways and other transitional elements stand out. Similarly, the lighting design utilizes highly efficient low-wattage fluorescent fixtures for work areas and architectural coves and turns to low-wattage quartz and metal halide sources to dramatize the art collection. James Musselman concludes his appraisal by declaring, "Our offices are spectacular."

Right: Island counter detail in multi-purpose room

Below: Employee's multi-purpose room

Ted Moudis Associates

Ted Moudis Associates

Financial Services Firm
New York, New York

Opposite top: Boardroom

Below: Reception and interconnecting stair

Right: Executive office

Far right: Executive lounge and meeting room

Bottom: Private office with detail of glass office fronts and millwork ceilings

Photography: Adrian Wilson Interior Photography

Ted Moudis Associates, once again, has demonstrated their ability to create a fresh new vision for this midtown financial services firm. The two-story, 18,400-square-foot space for 48 employees, designed by Ted Moudis Associates, creates an optimal work environment and provides the company with a dynamic and collaborative space reflecting their brand and culture. Two basic requirements are fulfilled by the design-delineating between two unique internal functions, and providing public and staff access to two key amenities, a grand outdoor terrace and a spectacular view of Central Park. At the same time it resolves interdepartmental adjacency flow, limited ceiling heights and small floor plates. The straightforward layout uses perimeter offices incorporating glass doors/fronts and clerestories to distribute daylight views and encourage staff interaction, as well as configures a conference suite so an adjacent pantry guarantees staff access to the terrace at all times. Because the firm wanted a setting that was "sleek yet warm," the design of the space is characterized by minimal modern forms, colors and textures, such as timeless materials in the form of limestone and cherry wood. A lighting design combining daylight and artificial lighting creates a boutique space with boundless vistas.

Ted Moudis Associates

Major League Baseball Advanced Media
New York, New York

Americans are particular about their favorite ballparks, and the new, one-floor, 14,000-square-foot office of Major League Baseball Advanced Media, the digital arm of the national pastime, evokes some of that unique passion for early 20th century stadiums. So the look of MLBAM's space in a New York City building, where it maintains other floors, shouldn't surprise any of its visitors. As designed by Ted Moudis Associates, the new floor houses nearly 100 employees in an industrial-style setting, derived in part from the building's original brick construction. Creating

an evocative image was not the only goal for a facility that comprises a reception/waiting area, private offices, conference room, bathrooms, pantry, breakout room and workstations. MLBAM sought a functional workplace that would be energetic and businesslike yet welcoming and comfortable while reinforcing its well-known brand. What visitors may not realize, of course, is the ambience needed special detailing. Besides exposing existing brick walls and ceiling vaults, the design added industrial style lighting and an exposed duct system that required raised openings

and additional structural supports. Everything is coordinated like teamwork, nonetheless, right down to the cool, contemporary furnishings, accented in red and blue to symbolize the game's place in our country's history, wood credenzas and work surfaces, carpet tile, and composite panels in open areas.

Above left: Reception seating area
Above right: Open office area
Right: Private office
Opposite: Conference room
Photography: Seth Boyd

Ted Moudis Associates

Cottingham & Butler
Dubuque, Iowa

One of the strongest abilities inherent in the profession of interior design is the talent to preserve the past, at the same time infusing new life in historic buildings, converting them into vibrant, modern environments that fuse the old with the new almost seamlessly. Ted Moudis Associates has done just that in downtown Dubuque, Iowa, taking the street level historical façade of a department store and joining it with a 20,000 square foot interior space that houses 74 employees of this insurance brokerage firm. Ornamental ironwork, refined finishes, and modern architectural forms assist in bridging the gap between old and new construction. Versatility in the layout encompasses multiple functional requirements of both private and interactive areas for staff and diverse formality levels of conference gathering. The inherent nature of the plan creates a hierarchy which steps from public to private to service areas as one walks through the office and moves deeper into the building's footprint. The base building is comprised of two older buildings with varied column spacing. The project required much coordination with local team members, inclusive of the landmark architect, historical commission, architect of record, lighting engineers, furniture dealer, millworker, and general contractor. Together with TMA, the team brought the project to fruition, updating Cottingham & Butler as a company founded rich with history yet progressive enough for the future, being led by the great grandson to the company's original founder.

Right, far right: Conference room, interconnecting stair leading to mezzanine

Below: Reception seating area with mezzanine beyond

Opposite top: Café integrated into feature wall

Opposite bottom: Open office area and feature wall

Photography: Eric Misko/Elite Images

Ted Moudis Associates

Société Générale
Chicago, Illinois

Ted Moudis Associates designed the interior space for Société Générale, France's second largest bank with US headquarters in New York, to house the firm's 32 employees within an icon of Chicago post-modern architecture, overlooking the downtown financial district. The results of the 11,500-square-foot office have a strong, branded identity that impresses visitors entering the space. Its high-end aesthetic design serves a variety of spatial experiences including open plan areas, common spaces for breaks and conferencing, as well as personal areas for individual offices including a unique boardroom with audio/visual qualities. The design team was able to capture the natural sunlight and provide a panoramic view through the private offices along the perimeter by designing a wood and glass office front, bringing sophistication and organization to the layout. Unique but unified materials work together to create a sense of office community with their other worldwide offices. The overall flow and progression of the space plan uplifted the firm's employee morale. Co-workers and teams now have improved communication and collaboration within their office, translating into an elevated sense of responsibility and ownership of their work environment, thus improving worker productivity.

Top: Unmanned reception area
Above: Conference room
Below left: Open office area

Below right: Pantry/break area
Photography: Darris Harris/ Padgett & Co.

TSC Design Associates, Inc.

275 Seventh Avenue, 19th Floor • New York, NY 10001 • 212.213.4595 • 212.213.8237 (F)

www.tscdesign.com

TSC Design Associates, Inc.

Weil Gotshal & Manges, LLP
Brooklyn, New York

Weil, Gothsal, & Manges LLP, a NYC based leading corporate law firm, decided to move 130 of its Manhattan support services employees to a one-floor, 30,000 square foot office in Brooklyn. To ensure a smooth transition from Manhattan to Brooklyn, the city's most populous borough, TSC Design engaged Weil, Gothsal, & Manges' end users in the design process. The result is a fresh approach to the traditional law office environment. An open floor plan was designed allowing for interaction between the staff. Private Offices were situated on the interior of the space, faced in clear glass, thus reducing the visual barriers and allowing natural light. The space also incorporates desirable modern amenities including a fitness center, cafe, lounge area, conferencing facilities, and training spaces. Weil, Gothsal, & Manges LLP also implemented sustainable practices in accordance with their corporate vision; water efficiency, lighting, materials and resources, indoor air quality, and access to public transportation were utilized to create a healthy work environment. As a result of these efforts, the space was awarded LEED Silver Certification from the United States Green Building Council and will remain a guideline for future workplace functions at Weil, Gothsal, & Manges LLP around the world.

Above right: Fitness center
Right: Reception
Below: Open area
Opposite: Café
Photography: Brian Rose

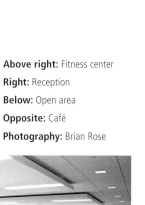

TSC Design Associates, Inc.

Financial Services Firm
New York, New York

Below: Pantry
Right: Open area
Bottom right: Executive office
Opposite: Reception
Photography: Brian Rose

The senior management of a New York-based Financial Services Firm retained TSC Design to create a space that showcased the firm's mission and blended with the high end area surrounding the space, which is located on 5th Avenue. The 11,000 sq space was design as an open floor plan, which allows for daylight to penetrate the space and for the occupants to take advantage of the NYC views. The majority of the space is open, with perimeter private offices encased in glass to keep the element of visual interaction throughout the space. The large executive office in situated in a corner which offers beautiful views but is also surrounded by glass partitions to allow the entire office to benefit from natural light. Teaming areas and a high end open pantry were created for impromptu meetings and spontaneous interactions between staff. A refined palate of materials, such as stone, walnut wood, upholstered panels and resins, provide a combination of warm and cool tones that create an environment which adheres to the nature of their financial business.

TSC Design Associates, Inc.

Vineyard Vines
Flagship Store
Greenwich, Connecticut

The team worked closely with Vineyard Vines to develop the concept of the 4,200 sf flagship store. The design of the store focused on the history of the Vineyard Vines brand, the philosophy of enjoyment of the "good life" and featuring their customers. A palette of white painted beadboard, reclaimed wood flooring, solid teak fixtures, white lacquered wood, boat hardware, nautical lighting and props all played a role in portraying the background of the brand. The fixtures were custom designed to evoke the "beachy" and "boaty" lifestyle, from a t-stand designed as a replica of the mast of a ship to the cash wrap created out of a life size custom Pearson boat hull. All of the store design incorporated authentic nautical details, elements and hardware. The overall store design helps draw customers into the store, inviting

them to stay longer, whether lingering in the home-like lounge area or reading the history of Vineyard Vines and customer profiles. It was the desire of the company's founders to create a space that was also flexible and useful for entertaining. The space has the ability to be transformed into an event space with local entertainment for Shep, Ian, the staff and Vineyard Vines patrons.

Above: View of main selling floor

Left: Exterior

Opposite top: Men's shirt and tie display

Opposite middle: Dressing rooms

Opposite bottom left: Lounge/waiting area

Opposite bottom right: Custom-designed T-stand

Photography: Whitney Cox

TSC Design Associates, Inc.

Dylan's Candy Bar Renovation
New York, New York

As the world's largest candy store, Dylan's Candy Bar has grown to become one of New York City's true sweet spots, sitting on the coveted list of top tourist attractions. But it's more than the Jelly Belly's, M&M's and chocolates galore that keep Dylan Lauren's throngs of candy fans returning to her 15,000 square-foot flavor haven on Manhattan's Upper East Side. The store's eclectic design is as central to its whimsical ambience as the sweets themselves. Dylan Lauren wanted to continue merging pop culture, art and fashion with candy, she tapped the New York-based design firm, TSC Design Associates, to expand and update her flagship store. The firm's sophisticated designs showcase the growth of her brand, with several new candy-themed offerings, including new branded environments to house her

evolving lifestyle brand and broadening the stores iconic imagery.

Upper ieft: Main sales floor featuring bulk bins

Upper right: Bulk bins, Chocolate the Bunny and cashwrap

Left: Chocolate World with dripping chocolate diplay

Above: Café area

Photography: Brian Rose

VOA Associates Incorporated

224 S. Michigan Avenue, Suite 1400 • Chicago, IL 60604 • 312.453.7793 • 312.554.1412 (F)

www.voa.com

VOA Associates Incorporated

MillerCoors Headquarters
Chicago, Illinois

The Miller Brewing Company (founded in 1855) and the Coors Brewing Company (founded in 1873), the nation's second and third largest beer breweries, have enjoyed a long and legendary rivalry. However, in 2007 a joint venture was formed by SABMiller and Molson Coors Brewing Company. The result: MillerCoors. The major design challenge for MillerCoors' eight-floor, 130,000 square foot headquarters was incorporating the history and heritage of both organizations in a dynamic new facility where personnel from the two former rivals could develop a new corporate culture. The Chicago location was chosen as a neutral city that was independent of Milwaukee, Wisconsin (Miller) and Golden, Colorado (Coors). The LEED Silver-certified design solution successfully combines the two breweries into a playful environment based on common goals for the new business. Like most

Above left: Corridor and kettle
Above right: "The Heart"
Right: Reception
Opposite: "Beer Land" stair
Photography: Nick Merrick/ Hedrich Blessing

VOA Associates Incorporated

headquarters, the new facility includes private offices, open workstations and conference spaces. Because it houses MillerCoors, however, the space also features an innovation laboratory, pub, and physical artifacts that tell the "stories" of the new partnership, including a copper brewing kettle, beer delivery truck, Cream City brick from the Milwaukee brewery, used to build the monumental stair connecting the 15th floor to the 16th floor pub, and the main bar in the pub, which references a traditional Chicago bar with its dark wood and brass accents. Such evocative design themes as "Beer Land" and "Brand Land" also help build the new corporate culture. "Beer Land," referring to the overarching company culture, is manifested through a similar layout and wayfinding path on each general floor anchored by "the Heart," a grouping of communal spaces, recycling center and copy center. Rising like a tree through all floors, "the Heart" glows amber and expresses the MillerCoors spirit through a super graphics wall; from this highly visible core, open workstations, conference areas, and café branch away. To foster camaraderie and build brand identity for MillerCoors products, including Miller Lite, Miller High Life, Miller Genuine Draft, Coors, Coors Light, Peroni, Blue Moon, Grolsch, and Leinenkugel to name a few, the design introduces a "Brand Land" environment on each general floor using a unique color palette, super graphics wall, café furniture, office furnishings and finishes that correlate to each brand's identity. Reviewing the fast-track project, which took just eight months from start to finish, MillerCoors CEO Leo Kiely recently commented, "The office is absolutely fabulous! You and your team and partners should be very proud. I get all kinds of positive comments. Mostly from jealous people."

Above and right: Pub
Far right: General offices
Opposite top left: Conference rooms
Opposite top right: Entry

VOA Associates Incorporated

VOA Associates
Chicago, Illinois

Facing a blank canvas in the form of raw space at Chicago's historic Santa Fe Railway Exchange Building--including the floor that once housed famed architect Daniel Burnham—the project team at VOA Associates Incorporated renovating the firm's existing, two-floor, 45,743-square-foot office embraced Burnham's admonition to "make no little plans." The driving theme for the design process would have delighted Burnham: an idea factory where employees can thrive, work and create. Combining thoughts of "how do we do our work" with "outcome," the project team shifted the design's emphasis to highlight process rather than end result. The new space consequently represents an open floor plan that promotes creativity, interaction and support for all kinds of media, appropriating the best Chicago has to offer, including spectacular natural light, cityscapes and lakefront views, while reinventing how architects and designers work. Every design detail helps reshape the practice. Main circulation pathways, for example, line the perimeter of workstations, conveying natural light

VOA Associates Incorporated

and views to all. Eliminating executive offices helps ease the transition from a traditional, buttoned-up setting of cubicles and corner offices to a universal, egalitarian space with large teaming areas as well as open workstations. Providing flexible team-ing areas that extend from the computer workstations allows project teams to produce models, mock-ups, vision boards and other collaborative efforts. An interior stair increases the connectivity between different studios while encouraging occupants to take the stairs. And as part of the sustainable design for which LEED Silver certification is pending, there are such green measures as recyclable building materials, stained MDF millwork, cork flooring, carpet with recycled content, and walls painted using low-VOC alternatives. If the new office is any indication, the firm founded in 1969 by Wilmont Vickrey, FAIA is more prepared than ever to deliver the remarkable service and award-winning design its clients expect.

Above far left: Collaborative Design area

Above left: Glass stair from the conference room

Left: Open Plan

Westgroup Designs, Inc.

Westgroup Designs, Inc.

Professional Hospital Supply
Temecula, California

PHS was founded in 1981 in Southern California, and is an independently woman-owned and operated company. From the very beginning, the company's vision was to continually strive to be the best and finest in the medical products supply industry. With sales forecast to exceed $850 million in 2010 and a collective workforce of 1700+, PHS is established as one of the nation's premier regional distributors. PHS has supported its remarkable growth in California with over 900,000 square feet of distribution, administrative and custom packaging facilities in Temecula, and a 212,000-square-foot distribution facility in Fairfield. These facilities provide full-line medical/surgical distribution services in California and Nevada. Additionally, PHS has full-service distribution centers in Phoenix, Arizona, Aurora, Colorado, Nampa, Idaho, and Salt Lake City, Utah to serve the western region of the United States. In October, 2009, PHS Corporate and Distribution opened their new; three story 600,000+ square foot Corporate Administration and Distribution facility in Temecula. All corporate officers are based at this facility as well as a full complement of administrative departments. This facility is open seven days a week, 24 hours a day, 365 days a year. The building of this remarkable structure represents a significant milestone in the company history and an extraordinary opportunity to service the customers from a truly state-of-the-art facility. This effort is the culmination

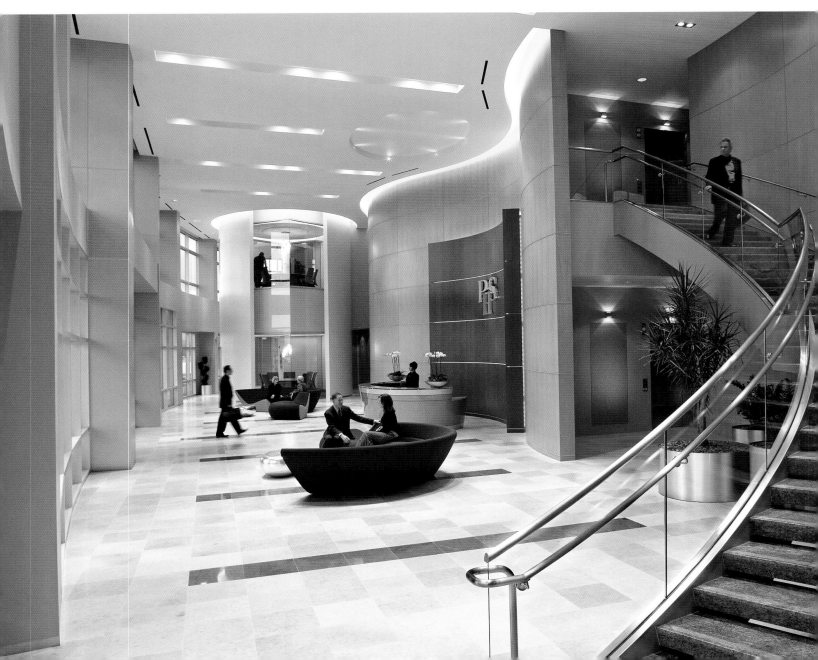

Above left: Conference room in main lobby

Above: Enclosure for main lobby conference rooms

Left: Reception desk

Far left: Main lobby

Photography: Michael Jarrett

Westgroup Designs, Inc.

of years of rigorous planning and development. PHS is focused on service, value and quality and provides such services as bulk distribution, just-in-time low unit of measure programs, and sterile custom procedure trays. Complementing this focus on the customer is

PHS's attention to the work environment for its employees in the company's new 80,000 square foot administrative offices, designed by Westgroup Designs, Inc. This freestanding office building, impressive as it is in its own right, is positioned on an elevated foothill alongside an

even larger, 530,000 square-foot warehouse. The challenge for the design team was to maximize exposure to natural light and scenic views of the mountains beyond, and to introduce flowing circulation spaces and definable operating zones. This promotes way-finding,

identity and intimacy of work area within the vast office space and the creation of dynamic visual elements for staff and visitors. As a result, this expansive contemporary facility is as inspiring as it is functional and efficient. The combining of quality materials as quarter-cut golden

and brown anigre wood, Emperador dark and light marble, Juparana granite, glass and stainless steel, and contemporary furnishings and a sophisticated lighting scheme of both direct and indirect lighting create these distinctive, elegant interiors. A consistently high level of

Above: Conference table in CEO office

Right: Executive restroom

Far right: CEO office

Opposite top: Bar/lounge in CEO office

Westgroup Designs, Inc.

stylish design characterizes the entire space comprised of reception areas, main lobby, inner lobbies, private offices, large open workstation zones, executive offices, boardroom, five conference rooms, training room, four lunch rooms, central computer IT zone and fitness center. Entering the main lobby, one is greeted by a

two-story, 25-foot-high space featuring a floating, curving grand staircase, custom designed reception desk, and two-story high ovoid-shaped glass conference enclosure, all enclosed by a gracefully curing exterior wall, a 25-foot tall serpentine, Anigre-covered interior wall. Hand-blown sculpted glass art mounted on the wall

behind a custom-designed executive desk, gives distinction to the CEO office, along with her private conference area, a formal seating area, and bar/lounge. A striking image is also created by the four custom-designed conference tables that dominate the boardroom, a spacious interior with a panoramic view, sculpted metal ceiling

and state-of-the-art AV technology. No less impressive is the design of the typical open workstations area, where a crisp, orthogonal furniture system of quarter-cut anigre wood and frameless glass panels contrasts with a curvilinear soffit encircling the area and mimicking the shape of adjacent corridors. Spectacular hand-blown,

wall-mounted art glass that lines the hallways of both second and third floor adds the visual interest to the hallway introducing vibrant accent color into their surroundings. The overall impact of the massively large structure is, unexpectedly, one of intimacy, warm finish, and sophisticated polish, technically advanced, efficient and

Top left: Executive waiting area

Left: Soft seating in executive office

Far left: Boardroom

Below: Executive office

filled with light within an exquisite natural setting- a facility that truly enhances the daily experience of the staff and visitors. The quality of the new facility is keenly appreciated by PHS, which commented, "Our goal was to achieve a workspace that withstood the test of time, from a design and functionality perspective. We feel that

Westgroup Designs, Inc.

the end result will not only allow us to efficiently service our current customers, but accommodate any growth over the next decade and beyond. Our architectural and design team went well beyond our expectations to deliver a facility that positions PHS for any challenge in the years to come. It is a true testament to the passion and commitment we bring to our industry."

Below left: Feature wall
Below: Workstation area
Below middle: Hallway

Bottom left: Training room
Bottom center: Lunch room
Bottom right: Lunch room

Wolcott Architecture Interiors

Wolcott Architecture Interiors

The Recording Academy
Santa Monica, California

The National Academy of Recording Arts and Sciences, better known as The Recording Academy, had requirements for its new, 300-person, three-floor, 66,000-square-foot office in Santa Monica that are not uncommon in commerical read estate; open, daylighted space, spacious lobby, many perimeter private offices, flexible layouts for meetings and special functions with a changing business model, stringent budget and sustainability. Despite potential incompatibility among its objectives, the success of the facility, designed by Wolcott Architecture Interiors, illustrates how careful planning, technical expertise and innovative design can overcome innumerable conflicts. Openness and private offices are accommo-dated with glass fronted corridor walls, doors and clerestory, while flexibility is maintained by movable walls, office furniture systems and other adaptable office components. Part of the second-floor slab has been removed to create a two-story lobby with a 20-foot-high water feature. Sliding glass doors facilitate indoor/outdoor meetings and after-hour functions. Extending the new base building's LEED Gold-certified conditions, the design incorporates green materials, energy-efficient lighting, and other design measures established by the entire project team to achieve a LEED Gold interior. Equally important for the Recording Academy, of course, is the quality of the workplace—warm, attractive and comfortable—for the

sponsor of the recording industry's Grammy Awards.

Right: Pivot doors from reception to front patio

Below: Reception, lobby and second floor lounge

Opposite lower left and right: Breakout area, corridor

Opposite bottom left: Main entrance

Photography: Marshall Safron

Wolcott Architecture Interiors

Beachbody
Santa Monica, California

Can private offices, open workstations, conference rooms, a film studio, editing bays, a fitness room, common areas and a kitchen/lounge coexist harmoniously within a largely open facility? It's all part of the workday for the 275 employees at Beachbody. The company is a popular producer of fitness and weight loss solutions that combine DVD-based in-home fitness programs with diet guidelines, nutritional supplements and interactive online support. The company's new, two-floor, 55,000-square-foot office in Santa Monica, designed by Wolcott Architecture Interiors, establishes an appropriately spacious and flexible workplace punctuated by blocks of acoustically conditioned private space to provide optimum working conditions. The design employs numerous techniques to balance the office environment, including carpet, sound-absorbent ceiling tile "clouds," upholstered walls, rubber flooring, sound-rated retractable wall systems, and double-pane interior glass to distribute daylight and views. The combination of these design elements simplify wayfinding and reconfiguring space while preserving visual and acoustic privacy. Not surprisingly, health is also essential to the new facility, as "green" materials, energy-efficient lighting and other sustainable features jointly create a sustainable office space, which attained LEED CI Gold certification to complement the overall LEED Gold-designated building. The integration of these elements provides a supportive workplace to serve such programs as Yoga Booty Ballet®, Slim in 6® and Turbo Jam®.

Right: Kitchen/pantry and flexible meeting space

Lower right: Window line circulation and workstations

Below: Reception lobby and kitchen/pantry

Photography: Marshall Safron

Wolcott Architecture Interiors

Karl Storz Endoscopy-America Inc.
El Segundo, California

Relocating from a space in Culver City, California that was dark, cluttered, and entangled in a maze of hallways to a new, airy, four-story, 85,000-square-foot office in nearby El Segundo dramatically transformed the image of Karl Storz Endoscopy-America, the U.S. sales and distribution affiliate of Karl Storz GmbH & Co., a world leader in advanced minimally invasive endoscopic technology and operating room integration solutions. The new U.S. headquarters, designed by Wolcott Architecture Interiors, strongly resembles its counterpart in Tuttlingen, Germany. However, its emphasis on openness, visibility, daylight and outdoor views required an internal task force to champion what the American staff perceived as drastic corporate culture changes. Thanks to thorough preparations for the move, the headquarters' 350 employees are delighted with the new private offices, open workstations, conference center, mock operating room, technology center, kitchen/lounge, data center and outdoor patio. The glass-enclosed private offices, open workstations with low panel heights, extensive use of glass throughout the interiors, and attractive contemporary furnishings give employees unprecedented opportunities to meet and interact in the branded facility. The life-enhancing, LEED Silver-certified environment surrounds them with sustainable materials, energy-efficient building systems, individual acoustical ceiling elements

Bottom left: Demonstration operatory

Below: View from top of stair facing history wall

Opposite top: Glass interconnecting stair

Photography: Marshall Safron

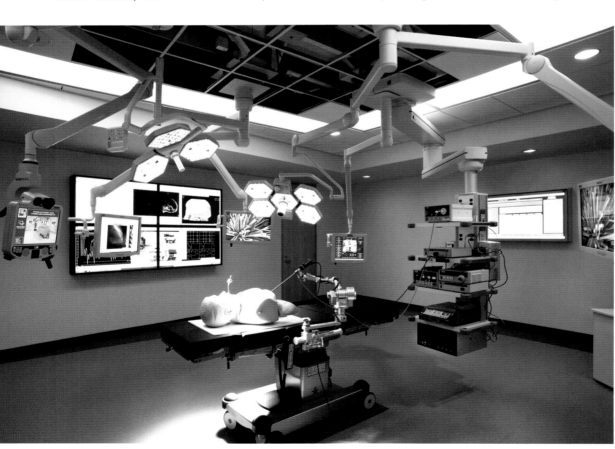

Wolcott Architecture Interiors

and individual lighting controls. Even customers notice the difference as soon as they enter the new space. The interior's fresh, European-style look places customers in a setting that is perfect for showcasing the company's state-of-the-art products. The interior plan establishes a carefully choreographed sequence leading from the reception area/lobby on the ground floor along a glass stair lined with a company "history wall" to the demonstration operatory and main video conference room upstairs. It's easy to see why one employee recently described the sleek composition in glass, aluminum and floor coverings as "inspiring."

Left: Staff dining room
Below: Main video conference room overlooking the stair

Lighting Designers

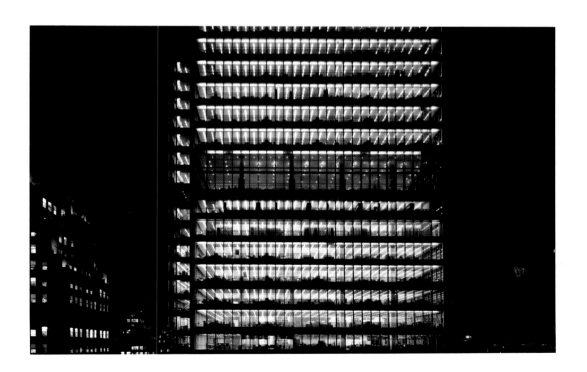

*A*lthough most employees of the corporate world observe some form of 9-to-5 workday, their employers are increasingly finding the workday never ends. The 24/7/365 environment of the global economy now continues uninterrupted, so that a project can be passed from one team to another—from New York to Los Angeles, Beijing, Frankfurt and back—as the world turns. Lighting has become a key environmental factor in this brave new world. Whether offices are open day or night, workers now process information in an expanding array of media whatever the illumination allows. The lighting design firms featured in the following pages can ensure that office workers view information in optimum conditions, whatever the hour or the medium.

Corporate Interiors No.10

Lighting Design Alliance

2830 Temple Avenue • Long Beach, CA 90806 • 562.989.3843 • 562.989.3847 (F)

Los Angeles • Chicago • Fort Collins • Dubai

www.lightingdesignalliance.com

Lighting Design Alliance

Lighting Design Alliance
Los Angeles, California

Top right: Exterior with main entrance

Right: Video conference room

Far right: Office area

Below: Employee lounge

Photography: RMA Architectural Photography

In a classic Cinderella-style transformation, Lighting Design Alliance has turned a dark, windowless warehouse in Long Beach, California once used to manufacture automobile wheel rims into a spacious, effective and inspiring lighting educational center for clients, architects and lighting design students as well as the Los Angeles office for its own staff. The transformation was all but inevitable, given that LDA is an internationally known lighting design firm actively involved with environmental design that chose to treat the conversion of the two-story, 20,000-square-foot facility as a special opportunity to practice what it preaches. Even so, the results are very impressive. Each element of the facility, designed by Lighting Design Alliance as lighting designer with design group Carl Ross as interior designer, functions as a showcase for new lighting technologies and techniques, Not only does it demonstrate nearly every new type of lighting technology on the market today, from the color-changing LED skylight to the solar-fed fiber optic accent lights, it fully integrates passive and active daylighting to sharply reduce energy consumption, making it one of the most energy-efficient buildings in California. Yet the renovated facility is also

Lighting Design Alliance

the product of careful thinking about its architecture and interior design. A generous, two-story-high entry with a soaring ceiling was added to the front of the existing structure, for example, to increase its scale and make it more inviting. Fifty-two skylights have been incorporated in the building, using triple-layered heat-stopping acrylic or double-paned low-e glass to maximize daylight and minimize heat gain. A bright central corridor equipped with a frosted acrylic ceiling system spans the entire length of the interior, from the lobby to the rear exit, illuminated by a clear, continuous skylight. An employee lounge featuring a billiard table, video games, and foosball tables is one of a number of popular staff amenities that offer respite from long hours of intensive work. At the same time, LDA's Los Angeles office represents an outstanding example of low-carbon-footprint real estate. With 100 percent daylight in work areas, photovoltaic panels, active sun tracking skylight and active daylight monitoring systems, daylight fiber-optic systems, electric lighting with full dimming and daylight harvesting capabilities and exterior solar shutters, the building is an incomparable testing laboratory for sustainability as well as an inspirational showcase of lighting design.

Right: Open plan workstations

Below right: Hallway

Bottom right: Conference room with nighttime lighting scheme

Below left: Reception

Lighting Design Alliance

Flashpoint
Chicago, Illinois

Below left: Ceiling at lobby
Below right: Lobby
Photography: Susan Carr/
©2007 Carr Cialdella Photography

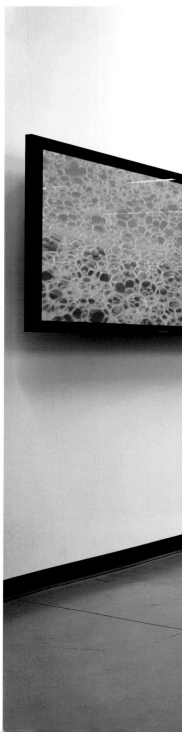

Historic Burnham Center may be a genuine landmark of Chicago architecture, but there is little hint of the past in the 32,000-square-foot Burnham Center campus of Flashpoint, The Academy of Media Arts and Sciences. An institution of higher learning offering two-year programs in the digital media arts entertainment industry, Flashpoint houses the majority of its classrooms and production facilities, including two sound stages, Apple Final Cut Pro and Avid Media Composer editing suites, multiple 2D/3D graphics compositing and game production workstations, and 5.1 surround sound audio mixing in the building at 28 North Clark Street, one of three locations it operates in the Windy City. The space is contemporary with futuristic touches, as could be expected, with a design by Lighting Design Alliance as lighting designer and Valeria Dewalt Train Associates as architect that smoothly integrates a battery of IT equipment

Lighting Design Alliance

with the school's various specialized environments. Appropriately, the lighting scheme is as up-to-date as any other technological feature. Classrooms, for example, have a combination of narrow aperture linear fluorescents with perimeter wall washers to provide functional lighting with minimal glare to support computer-oriented tasks, and combine daylight harvesting sensors on the perimeters with occupancy sensors to dim the fluorescents to achieve automatic energy savings. In the lobby, ceiling surface-mounted linear fluorescent downlights are complemented by LED linear striplights to deliver a cohesive design statement that is both functional and timely. Everywhere they go at the Burnham Center campus, students are thus reminded that state-of-the-art lighting is part of experiencing the digital media arts at their best.

Above and left: Classrooms illuminated for computer-oriented tasks

SBLD Studio

SBLD Studio

DLA Piper U.S., LLP
Washington, D.C.

With the arrival of DLA Piper LLP., an eight floor, 230,000 square foot speculative office building in Washington DC, has become the single occupant home of the newest US office of DLA Piper, one of the world's largest law firms, with 3500 lawyers in over 65 offices in the Europe, Asia, Africa and the Middle East. As interior architects for the project, Lehman-Smith + McLeish proposed modifications to the base building to produce a striking contemporary environment; by recapturing the ground floor lease space the project was able to achieve a dedicated street level entry, a large high ceiling conference center, and vertical atrium with multiple open balconies. Lighting was critical to the overall success of DLA Piper's new offices. As lighting designers, SBLD Studio were able to maximizing available light from the skylights by adding light sources directed at the available surfaces in the voluminous atrium to create a bright and welcoming environment in the lobby as well as in the offices and conference rooms adjacent to the atrium as it ascends the building. While the lighting elsewhere in the building may not be as dramatic as the glow in the public spaces, it is critical in making DLA Piper's award winning new home come alive.

Above: Lobby
Above right: Conference room
Below: Dining room
Below right: Servery
Opposite: Atrium
Photography: Jim Tetro

SBLD Studio

New York Times Headquarters
New York, New York

The New York Times Company program mandated 700,000+ sq. ft. of predominantly open-office area that emphasized communication, collaboration and transparency which lead to the development of a lighting design solution that is environmentally responsive and flexible with maximum daylighting penetration, including a sophisticated lighting control and shading system. The exterior porcelain rods block a significant amount of direct sunlight penetration while the floor to ceiling highly transparent clear glass allows an abundance of daylight. The mechanized shading system is automatically deployed to maximize visual comfort and mitigate sunlight infiltration and excessive glare. In coordination with the interior designers, SBLD's custom ceiling system incorporates fluorescent sources with digital dimming ballasts, air return, occupancy sensors and photocells with its recessed troffers. The digital addressable ballasts satisfy the Client's dual requirement for daylight harvesting, with continuous dimming and flexibility to reconfigure space to meet ever changing business requirements. This custom ceiling and lighting system is repeated on the podium floors with additional automated horizontal louvers to control daylight penetration at the skylights. Typical elevator lobbies are used as an exhibition space for archival newspaper prints. Halogen accent lights and

direct-indirect fluorescent sources are used. In the cafeteria, the halogen lights are dimmed during the daylight hours. Both the electric lighting and shading system were completely commissioned by the system manufacturer and tested thoroughly by an independent institution and have been monitored carefully by the owner. This innovative and sustainable lighting design solution achieves an energy savings of 70% the building's 1.28 w/sq.ft. connected load.

Above: Conference room

Left: Exterior at night

Far left: Newsroom

Opposite top left: Entrance to conference room

Opposite top right: Gallery

Photography: Nic Lehoux

SBLD Studio

Bingham McCutchen Boston Headquarters
Boston, Massachusetts

Because the 12-floor, 320,000-square-foot Boston headquarters for 300 attorneys of Bingham McCutchen, a major law firm with offices in the United States, United Kingdom, Hong Kong and Japan, is split between two different elevator banks, the facility designed by Lehman Smith McLeish, as architect, and SBLD Studio, as lighting designer, established two vertically integrated hubs to encourage interaction. The upper level hub serves client entry and meetings with reception and conference rooms, while the lower level hub houses dining, training and multi-purpose facilities. Since Bingham McCutchen sought a bright, animated and contemporary space, multi-story spaces have been carved from existing floors to add volume and drama, and lighting is designed to heighten visual impact. Conference center reception area lighting is ethereal, for example, wrapping glowing frosted glass interior walls around three of four sides, backlit by fluorescent slots, to complement daylight entering one two-story window wall. This high ambient environment extends throughout much of the facility. In the main auditorium and cafeteria, glowing L-shaped bars, incorporating fluorescent strips behind white diffusers, provides general illumination and architectural form. Taut ceilings with fluorescent strips and halogen downlights, as well as ceiling and floor coves, help complete the design's modernistic image.

Far left: Reception
Left: Cafeteria
Lower far left: Auditorium
Lower left: Servery
Photography: John Miller © Hedrich Blessing

SBLD Studio   Tishman Speyer Headquarters
New York, New York

Tishman Speyer is one of the world's leading owners, developers, operators, and managers of first class real estate worldwide, managing a portfolio of assets of over 116 million square feet of domestic and international commercial space. Appropriately, the company's 65,000 sq.ft. headquarters is located on three floors in Rockefeller Center, arguably,

one of the most iconic buildings in mid-town Manhattan. The classically clean lines of their new offices designed by Lehman-Smith McLeish, serve as the perfect backdrop for their extensive avant garde art collection. In fact, the architecture and lighting of the facility which includes reception, private offices and open workstation areas, conference rooms and galleries

joined by an interconnecting stair, work in perfect harmony to enhance the masters of contemporary art on display throughout the space. To create the museum-like volume amidst the low ceiling in the historic 45 Rock, the floors were removed in several areas to form multistory volumes that integrate the art seamlessly throughout the public areas and

illuminates the art and architecture with both natural and artificial light. The ambient illumination, designed by SBLD Studio, is provided by backlit fluorescent ceiling fixtures and wall elements to resemble daylight streaming in the rooms, while focal light from halogen track lighting uniquely defines each art piece. Surrounded by one of America's great 20th Century

landmarks, the office offers as much to see inside as well as outside.

Above left: Entry lobby
Above: Reception desk
Below left: Conference break-out room
Below: Corridor
Photography: © Peter Aaron/ Esto Photographics

SBLD Studio

BBH
New York, New York

Advertising agencies are in the business of interesting you in something you may or may not need by making you believe you cannot possibly manage without it. Gensler, the interior designers for BBH's offices, used some slick marketing techniques to convince the client that the long collaborative workstations, à la financial institution's trading desks, were just the thing to promote the interactive dynamic environment that is key to these ad wizards that started in the UK in 1982 working out of their briefcases. Today their 42,000 sq. ft. New York office designed by Gensler, as interior designer, with SBLD Studio, as lighting designers, is structured similarly to BBH's London headquarters. The open plan office with an "out of the box" lighting concept provides the agency's hip, young staff with a work environment to match their dynamic creative approach to advertising. The challenge for the lighting scheme was to sustain the sense of cutting edge excitement across a facility that includes private offices, open workstations, A/V conference facilities, design production areas, and a café/coffee bar area. SBLD Studio's solution introduces a rich variety of creative techniques. From the suspended "threads of light" supporting bare bulbs at varying heights in the reception area, to the fluorescent bars and industrial pendants integrated into the upper ceiling with it's exposed structure and duct work that lights the work areas. The staff of BBH experience light as both a noun and a verb.

Below left: Team in open work area
Below: Open workstations
Bottom left: Café/coffee bar
Bottom: Reception
Photography: Andrew Bordwin Photographer

A Directory of Legacy Design Firms

*T*o celebrate the publication of the 10th volume of Corporate Interiors, Visual Profile Books has invited the architecture and interior design firms that have consistently appeared in past volumes to join us in telling the corporate world why business needs design in the fiercely competitive global economy of the digital age.

These design professionals represent some of the nation's most talented, experienced and innovative firms. In the pages that follow, they introduce themselves, their projects and other accomplishments, and show how they can help your organization to succeed today. Each presentation includes contact information to facilitate detailed inquiries.

Corporate Interiors invites the leaders of businesses and institutions to consider the services of these design firms, as well as all those whose work appears in the preceding pages, as you develop important facilities of your own. The stakes have never been higher. These firms can give you workplace environments custom designed to helps your people put your corporate strategies to work.

Corporate Interiors No.10

AECOM

515 South Flower Street, Level 8 • Los Angeles, CA 90071 • 213.593.8300

800 Douglas Entrance • North Tower, 2ⁿᵈ Floor • Coral Gables, Florida 33134 • 305.444.4691

2777 East Camelback Road, Suite 200 • Phoenix, AZ 85016 • 602.337.2700

3101 Wilson Blvd, Suite 900 • Arlington, VA 22201, USA • 703.682.4900

10 South Jefferson Street, Suite 1600 • Roanoke, VA 24011 • 540.857.3100

448 Viking Drive, Suite 145 • Virginia Beach, VA 23452 • 757.306.4000

Americas • Europe • Asia • Middle East • Africa • Australia • New Zealand

www.aecom.com

At AECOM, we seek a balance between art and technology, form and function, beauty and purpose, vision and result. Our architects and interior design professionals have helped shape the world around us, from high-rise buildings that form city skylines, to educational, cultural, research and transportation facilities that enable our way of life and future.

Problem solvers by nature, we serve clients by listening to their concerns, understanding their goals, and sharing in their vision. We believe that capital investments in facilities should be aligned with measurable, sustainable business benefits, and our portfolio reflects a commitment to excellence and client satisfaction. Sustainability is synonymous with good design, and principles of environmental awareness are fundamental to our design culture and integral to every discipline. For each building type, our design process is based on energy efficient building systems, appropriate selection of materials and form to maximize environmental conditions and long term performance. Our sustainable solutions have shaped projects such as the Calgary Courts Centre in Alberta, Canada, Altria Group Headquarters and Annex in Virginia, United States and the Rand Corporation in California, United States. United States. Throughout the world, our projects have achieved honors and recognition for environmental responsibility.

We create environments to work, collaborate, learn, relax and inspire. AECOM's interiors team is recognized for designing appropriate environments for clients across all market sectors and for bringing a new approach to traditional challenges. Our projects range from Fortune 100 company headquarters to boutique hotels to interiors for public agencies. In each of our projects, we act as stewards of our clients' aspirations and fiscal realities, working to capture opportunities and plan for the long term.

Mancini•Duffy

39 West 13th Street • New York, NY 10011 • T : 212.938.1260 • 800.298.0868 • F : 212.938.1267
New York • New Jersey • Connecticut • Wasshington DC • London UK
www.manciniduffy.com • info@manciniduffy.com

As an architecture and design firm, this is our mission: to make each client a client for life. We know that it's the collaboration of the client and our team that drives the success of each project. We are creators who place people at the center of our work, and we carry out our mission through quality, professionalism, and service—and a leadership that believes in the greatness of our team. We make it a priority to find, train, and empower the people who are Mancini•Duffy, and give them the tools they need to excel at their work. Delivering excellence to our clients, our mission is to earn the right to be called their trusted advisor.

Kishimoto Gordon Dalaya PC

1300 Wilson Boulevard, Suite 250 • Rosslyn, VA 22209 • T : 202.338.3800 • F : 703.749.7998
www.kgdarchitecture.com

Kishimoto Gordon Delaya PC is an architectural, interiors, and planning firm based in the Washington, DC metropolitan area that provides design services in national and international markets. Our efficient and integrated design process creates high-quality, market driven designs that give clients a competitive edge in their business to succeed in tomorrow's marketplace.

KGD's commitment to quality has resulted in numerous design awards in recognition of design excellence and environmental stewardship. Our experience includes: commerical and corporate office, retail, mixed use, high-rise residential, institutional, and sustainable design projects.

JPC Architects

601 108th Ave NE, Suite 2250 • Bellevue, WA 98004 • T : 425.641.9200 • F : 425.637.8200
www.jpcarchitects.com

Our doors opened in 1986 in Redmond, Washington with a primary focus on interior architecture and design. We have evolved into one of the largest design firms in the Pacific Northwest providing building design, interior architecture, and facilities management services. Corporate, retail, medical, and dental projects are the foundation of our portfolio. Our collective team of architects, interior designers, technical staff, and construction managers share a commitment to meeting the business objectives of our clients while crafting inspirational, sustainable, and productive workplaces.

H. Hendy Associates

4770 Campus Drive • Newport Beach, CA 92660 • T : 949.851.3080 • F : 949.851.0807
www.hhendy.com

Our commitment is to create intelligent environments that will allow our clients to realize today's business potential and unlock tomorrow's promises.

Our belief is that success begins with listening and understanding our client's business objectives and cultural values. We achieve success through our creative intellect, seamless communication and proven project control – in other words, exceptional service! For over 25 years, H. Hendy Associates has provided innovative interior architectural services to clientele nationally. Our clients include corporate, finance, legal, high tech, and retail leaders of American business. Rated in the top 200 design firms since 1983, we offer a full spectrum of services from strategic planning, office planning, and creative design to construction services; post occupancy evaluation and facilities management.

H. Hendy Associates makes it easy to do business. We have an entrepreneur culture that is horizontal and centered around our clients. We stay focused on our clients and their industry demands. Constantly meeting and anticipating their needs for now and in the future.

Our people are our strength, as their creative talent, business acumen and technical competence are the keystones to our success. H. Hendy Associates stretches the creative boundaries of each project with fresh approaches based on our vast experience, through research and endless imagination. We organize our architects, programmers and interior designers into permanent teams, each led by a firm principal to ensure continuity throughout each project. Driven to continuously raise the bar of excellence, our teams maintain the highest standards of professionalism and commitment at every level.

Gensler

Abu Dhabi • Atlanta • Austin • Baltimore • Beijing • Boston • Charlotte • Chicago • Dallas • Denver • Detroit • Dubai • Houston
La Crosse • Las Vegas • London • Los Angeles • Minneapolis • Morristown • New York • Newport Beach • Phoenix • San Diego
San Francisco • San José, Costa Rica • San Jose • San Ramon • Seattle • Shanghai • Singapore • Tampa • Tokyo • Washington, DC
www.gensler.com

As architects, designers, planners and consultants, we partner with our clients on some 3,600 projects every year. These projects can be as small as a wine label or as large as a new urban district. With more than 2,300 professionals networked across 33 offices, we serve our clients as trusted advisors, combining localized expertise with global perspective wherever new opportunities arise.

Our work reflects an enduring commitment to sustainability and the belief that design is one of the most powerful strategic tools for securing lasting competitive advantage.

Francis Cauffman

New York • Philadelphia • Baltimore
www.franciscauffman.com

Francis Cauffman is a source of new ideas for positive change. We work cooperatively with our clients to conceptualize and realize new futures. Using state-of-the-art technologies, we develop imaginative and sustainable projects that are loved by the people who use them. We enjoy this process, and we embrace it.

Our professionals have broad expertise and deep industry resources. We provide architecture, interior design, and planning services in four major areas of focus: healthcare, corporate, science and technology, and government and justice. We help our clients to make astute and strategic decisions that help them leverage their real estate for lasting, long-term value.

Conant Architects

Madison Avenue • New York, NY 10017 • T : 212.672.2862 • F : 646.865.1377
w.conantarchitects.com

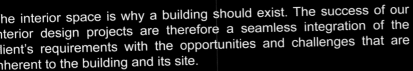

he interior space is why a building should exist. The success of our interior design projects are therefore a seamless integration of the client's requirements with the opportunities and challenges that are inherent to the building and its site.

A singular idea needs to evolve from the needs and aspirations of the client along with the uniqueness of the building envelope and site condition.

Our projects seek to reflect our commitment to outstanding design and our client's long term success.

Our process is one of gathering information, analysis and clear formulation of a plan. Whether we are determining the size, location, budget or cultural message of a project, it all begins with knowing what information is required. In some cases we will specifically compare the client's needs with others of a smiliar nature. At other times we work to determine the uniqueness and clarity that will distinguish the end results.

In all cases, our projects encompass the client's long term individual

Aref & Associates was founded to meet the space planning and interior design needs of major corporations, professional service firms and developers. Our basic philosophy as a boutique design firm is to establish a long term working relationship with our clients based on a clear understanding of their design objectives and corporate identity, and ultimately create an intelligent working environment to meet those objectives and identity.

Over the years, our success has been attributed to the development of strategic planning concepts adhering to our basic design philosophy of form follows function. In essence, we create innovative solutions efficiently and economically that specifically address our client's long-term requirements. This philosophy balances the pragmatic climate that exists in the global economy with a strong commitment to high quality design.

The success of a boutque design firm lies in the collaborative effort of the design team and its commitment to hands-on

approach by the principals of the firm to all aspects of the planning and design process. As a team, we review and analyze out client's design criteria and propose solutions that are on the cutting edge of design that lead to the development of a new environment within a design concept that allows form to follow function.

As a highly motivated design firm, we are able to become involved in a select number of quality projects that allow out principals to bring hands-on involvement at each step of the design pricess. Thus, our clients are provided with the highest level of professional services that they deserve and have come to trust.

This philosophy and approach has led to the many long-term relationships we have built over the years and will continue to provide the foundation for our success as we move to cyberspace in the 21st century.

Margulies Perruzzi Architects

308 Congress Street • Boston, MA 02210 • T : 617 482 3232
www.mp-architects.com

Margulies Perruzzi Architects is one of Boston's largest architecture and interior design firms, and has been in business for more than 20 years. The firm specializes in serving clients for whom the workplace is an important part of their business—specifically in the Corporate, Healthcare, Real Estate Development, Professional Services, and Research and Development communities.

Our team of talented architects and interior designers use an interactive design approach and cutting-edge technology to integrate the input of those who will use the space into every aspect of the design.

Margulies Perruzzi Architects has designed more than million square feet of space, and is proud to maintain man longstanding client relationships. Some of the firm's client include Blue Cross Blue Shield of Massachusetts, Covidien Forrester Research, and Liberty Mutual.

MKDA

902 Broadway, 17th Floor • New York, NY 10010 • T : 212.532.9800 • F : 212.889.2180
www.mkda.com

MKDA is a leading corporate space planning, interior design and consulting firm headquartered in New York City with a second office in Stamford, CT. Since its inception in 1959, MKDA has earned a strong reputation for its commitment to exceptional client service and its proven expertise in interior planning and design.

The firm creates award-winning interiors for an array of corporate space users and commercial building owners, optimizing interior environments to meet each client's unique real estate requirements and business objectives.

Whether executing a renovation, expansion, or retrofit, MKDA workspaces reflect the unique brand identities of its clients. As such, MKDA has been engaged by companies ranging in size from start-up ventures to established global brands in numerous U.S. markets. Its corporate clients span the finance, insurance, legal, new media, education and retail sectors, to name a few.

MKDA was one of the first interiors firms to incorporate project management into its services, and its remains a leader in this field. From inception through completion, the design firm manages each project with the utmost attention to budgets and schedules.

In addition, the firm is noted for its real estate market expertise. MKDA works closely with clients and their agents to provide comprehensive spatial analysis and design from the onset of space search through project completion. With this expertise, MKDA has also created a solid niche creating "built" environments, assisting commercial building owners in leasing space.

With a commitment to sustainability, and answering the market's demand for "green" environments, MKDA employs LEED-accredited professionals who source the latest in attractive, durable and economical sustainable materials and systems.

MKDA has spent decades earning its reputation, one client at a time. It consistently exceeds expectations to win repeat and referral business, allowing the firm to stand apart from its competitors.

M Moser Associates

14/F North Somerset House, Taikoo Place, 979 King's Road • Quarry Bay, Hong Kong
T : 852.3665.2251 • F : 852.2806.1403
www.mmoser.com

M Moser creates design concepts that perform as business solutions for our Clients. We integrate a company's business requirements, image, and staff needs with advanced workplace strategies and design that are flexible, technology responsive, and quickly delivered at the right price and at appropriate quality levels.

We are focused on maximizing our Client's investment in their premises and the people they serve by offering services that add value to that investment.

At M Moser our designs do more than provide our Client's with a beautiful work space. Our designers are experts in furniture and material selection and in the coordination of information technologies, telephony technologies and building services technologies that are the heart of a world class workplace.

Mojo•Stumer Associates, P.C.

14 Plaza Road • Greenvale, NY 11548 • T : 516.625.3344 • F : 516.625.3418
www.MOJOSTUMER.com

Mojo•Stumer, from its inception has been designed to be unique, combining quality architecture and interior design with complete project management systems.

Founded in 1980 by two partners who came from design backgrounds, the firm quickly grew and established itself as a leader in the design field and one of the most highly respected architectural firms in the country. Since its founding, the firm has won over 60 national and regional architectural and interior design awards and has been widely published in national and international books, periodicals and newspapers.

Since its founding, the firm has worked on a variety of different building types. For all of these building types, we have provided to our clients comprehensive master planning, architecture and total interior design, while also incorporating the best consultants in structural engineering, mechanical engineering, and landscape architecture. Our over 20 years of experience and the constant search for more creative solutions has enabled us to stay on the cutting edge of design. The attention to our client's program, respecting the importance of their budgets while still searching for the right solution to create an exciting environment has been instrumental in our firm's success.

Montroy Andersen DeMarco Design Inc.

99 Madison Avenue, 14th Floor • New York, NY 10016 • T : 212.481.5900 • F : 212.481.7481
www.montroyandersendemarco.com • info@madgi.com

Founded in 1990, Montroy Andersen is an interior design firm with a contemporary philosophy, offering cutting edge space within an established budget. The principals are listeners who are focused on achieving the client's vision. Their values have penetrated the firm at all levels, creating a client focused group of professionals.

As the firm has grown, one very important thing has not changed: First-hand principal attention to each commission is still a key element of the process. This attention has enabled the firm to develop a group of legacy clients who speak for the firm. They recommend the firm to their colleagues and return with new assignments.

Montroy Andersen provides a wide range of architectural, interior design and project management services. Client requirements and location specifics create the exact scope of services.

Founded in 1976, MSA planning + design is a private, women-owned planning, design, and architecture firm with offices in San Francisco and Seattle. We provide innovative, effective consulting and design services for a wide range of clients, focusing on workplace, retail, healthcare, and hospitality. MSA is dedicated to providing creativity and responsiveness rooted in a thorough understanding of each client's culture, goals, and values. Our experienced staff brings focus, technical expertise, and fiscal responsibility to every project, from inception to completion. We establish and maintain working relationships based on trust and integrity that enable our clients to make fully informed decisions during each phase of the design and construction process.

Every company likes to think it's unique, but most are just variations on a theme. NELSON is different. You can feel it in our integrated services infrastructure that offers a single-source solution for facilities-oriented needs. You can see it in our design vision as we create spaces that deliver on client desires, support their objectives and delight the users. You can hear it as our Teammates collaborate with clients and one another to create strategies and plans that optimize facilities, support technology needs, incorporate sustainability and LEED certification, reflect corporate cultures and impact the way people work.

We accomplish all this by forming true partnerships with our clients to thoroughly understand every detail of their needs, objectives, timelines and budgets. We then utilize the resources of our six lines of business—Interior Design, Architecture, Strategies, Workplace Services, Engineering and Information Services—along with our network of national and global locations, subject matter experts, and combined knowledge of industry trends and best-in-class practices—to create and execute solutions that truly add value.

The NELSON name has been synonymous with quality and leadership for more than 32 years. We continue to find new ways to grow, improve and innovate – all to the benefit of our clients. We're very proud to be ranked in the Top Two firms specializing in corporate interiors (*Interior Design Magazine* 2010 Giants). Looking to the future, we will continue to embrace our motto—Focused on Creation, Passion to Deliver—and build on our industry position, discover new ways to bring value to our clients, and provide anytime / anywhere service in the most efficient, effective and beneficial ways possible.

OWP/P | Cannon Design

111 West Washington Street, Suite 2100 • Chicago, IL 60602 • 312.960.8032 • 312.332.9601 (F)
www.cannondesign.com

Cannon Design is an Ideas Based Practice, ranked among the leading international firms in planning and design for healthcare, science & technology, education, sports & recreation, commercial and government clients. At present, the firm employs a staff of over 1,000, delivering services in 17 offices throughout North America, as well as abroad in Shanghai, China, and Mumbai, India.

Cannon Design's practice is based upon the philosophy of comprehensive service, providing our clients with a single point of responsibility. By bringing architecture, interior design and engineering together in a single organization, we ensure efficient and effective service. Conceptually, we believe the building sciences of architecture and engineering cannot be separated. Engineering is an integral part of building design, providing the technological framework that transforms architectural concept into a safe, comfortable and functional place, efficient to operate and easy to maintain.

Our mission is to plan and design buildings and their interiors that promote productivity, enhance the quality of life of users and visitors and contribute value to the environment. We believe good design is the physical expression of sound ideas, imagination and creativity. Rather than work from a predetermined approach, we strive to create environments that are a thoughtful response to their program mission, physical setting and functional purpose. A guiding principle of Cannon Design is that each project reflects the spirit and personality of its owner.

Westgroup Designs

19772 MacArthur Blvd, Suite 100 • Irvine, CA 92612 • T : 949.250.0880 • F : 949-250-0882
www.westgroupdesigns.com

Great design is always a process driven by experienced insight and skillful, creative leaps fueled by passion. In the most fundamental way, the design process always contains the seemingly simple components: a program, a building resulting from the context of its site and the final interior world created for the everyday use and enjoyment of the occupants. The success and specialness of that interior world can truly impact its users by giving them an efficient, functional and visually uplifting place for their use. Achieving that is a primary goal of Westgroup.

Westgroup Designs' is successful in advancing and fulfilling the design process and achieving owner's goal while exceeding their expectations. Westgroup brings a special level of detail to its vision and to the architecture by creating an atmosphere born from applying intimate knowledge of finishes, furniture, equipment and lighting married to an in-depth understanding of required functions and shaped through their masterful skill of organizing spatial flow for today's automated world. These worlds are brought to life through the latest computer technology of Building Information Modeling guided by pure individual artistic creativity, an understanding of building systems and founded in an Owner's needs.

Excellence in design is fundamental to Westgroup as a visionary partnership nurturing an active, working relationship with its clients in order to achieve the highest and best goals and solutions—that is Westgroup Designs' legacy: beautiful, uplifting, functional spaces for a satisfied client.

Wolcott Architecture + Interiors

3869 Cardiff Avenue • Culver City, California • T : 310.204.2290 • F : 310.838.6109
www.wolcottai.com

Wolcott has the professional expertise and resources to engage projects of any magnitude. Reinforced by principal involvement from project inception to completion, this commitment to excellence is reflected in a high percentage of referral and repeat business.

Design and Project Management Services:

* Architecture / Planning
* Programming / Building Evaluation
* Space Planning / Conceptual Design
* Design Development
* Sustainable Design (LEED)
* Construction Documentation
* Bidding / Negotiations and Award
* Construction Administration / Observation
* Post-Construction

Index by Project